ALABAMA: Robert Irving was working under his truck when his young son felt a gentle touch and a soft voice told him to place a piece of wood under the truck's bumper. No sooner had he done so when the jack slipped. "My God," Robert Irving said. "How'd you know that jack was going to fall?"

COLORADO: Earl and Ted were climbing a 13,000-foot peak near Rocky Mountain National Park. While Earl was catching a nap, Ted explored the view. Suddenly, he lost his footing and slipped! Hanging by his fingertips, he screamed to his friend, but to no avail. Suddenly, Ted felt strong hands grip his faltering wrists and looked up to see a stranger, who effortlessly pulled him to safety . . . and disappeared.

HAWAII: Matthew and his wife, Barbara, were scuba diving in Hawaii. When Barbara came up to prepare their picnic lunch, Matthew continued to explore. Suddenly, a stranger approached her and said, "Barbara, your husband is in trouble." Grabbing her air tank Barbara dove, and found her husband laying on the bottom, doubled over in pain. Her quick action saved his life . . . but Barbara knew it was God's messenger who helped her.

The Complete Angel:
Angels Through the Ages—
All You Need to Know

Other Avon Books by
James N. Pruitt

ANGELS BESIDE YOU

The Complete Angel

ANGELS THROUGH THE AGES— ALL YOU NEED TO KNOW

JAMES N. PRUITT

AVON BOOKS ◆ NEW YORK

All Scripture quotations unless otherwise noted are from the King James or Authorized version of the Bible.

Grateful acknowledgment is made to the following for permission to reprint previously published material: excerpts from *Where Angels Walk* by Joan Webster Anderson, Barton & Brett; *Guidepost* Magazine, Guidepost Associates, Inc., Carmel, New York 10512; excerpts from *Know Your Angels* by John E. Ronner, Mamre Press, 107 South Second Avenue, Murfreesboro, Tennessee 37130, reprinted by permission; *The White Dog* by Neva Joyce Coil, copyright © 1993 by Guidepost Associates, Inc.

THE COMPLETE ANGEL: ANGELS THROUGH THE AGES—ALL YOU NEED TO KNOW is an original publication of Avon Books. This work has never before appeared in book form.

AVON BOOKS
A division of
The Hearst Corporation
1350 Avenue of the Americas
New York, New York 10019

Copyright © 1995 by James Pruitt
Published by arrangement with the author
Library of Congress Catalog Card Number: 94-96432
ISBN: 0-380-78045-3

First Avon Books Printing: April 1995

AVON TRADEMARK REG. U.S. PAT. OFF. AND IN OTHER COUNTRIES, MARCA REGISTRADA, HECHO EN U.S.A.

Printed in the U.S.A.

RA   10 9 8 7 6 5 4 3 2 1

Contents

Introduction

THIS BOOK IS the result of nearly ten months of research, phone conversations, and interviews with people just like you and me. What makes these people so special are the stories they have to tell of an experience not everyone has had—an encounter with angels.

I first became interested in the study of the stories of angelic happenings while watching a television special almost two years ago. Skeptical at first, I figured these people had experienced something, but that in a time of great stress or danger a person's adrenaline is rushing and it is easy to mistake a narrow miss or a certain occurrence which averts danger as some type of miracle. But then, the longer I thought about it, the more I knew that I was no different from those I had been quick to judge.

My thoughts slipped back to Vietnam and a number of strange things I had seen and heard that had no explanation. A bullet going through a man's helmet and coming out without leaving a scratch anywhere on the man's head. A boy leapt on a grenade, but it failed to go off. When we walked away five minutes later, the same grenade exploded.

Those were the type of things I began to think about. Were those miracles or luck? Had these people been just lucky or had they been saved by their guardian angels? I found the questions intriguing. So much so, that I began to research the association of angels and war. The result was my book, *Angels Beside You*, published by Avon Books in December 1994. It verified my suspicions—angelic experiences had been encountered in every war known to man.

I became a loyal fan of Sophy Burnham's *A Book of Angels* and *Angel Letters*, of Joan Webster Anderson's *Where Angels Walk* and, of course, of John Ronner's *Do You Have a Guardian Angel?* These writers served as an inspiration for me during my work on *Angels Beside You*.

One day at work someone asked how many angels I could name. I quickly stated that I could name a considerable number of them. That considerable number came to a total of—four!

I must admit, for a person who had just written a book on angels in war, I was embarrassed. Then I found there was hardly anyone who could name even four! Thus came the idea for an encyclopedia of angels. After all, Oral Roberts University was just down the road in Tulsa. Oklahoma Baptist University wasn't that far away, and of course, I had Oklahoma University right next door. With all those sources available for research, it could be done—or so I thought.

Eight months later, and having exhausted my resources, I could only come up with enough names to fill fifty pages. Not exactly the size book my publisher had in mind at the time we closed the deal. Then I happened to see a newspaper story about an incident in Alaska that had all the markings of angelic intervention. Two days later, another story emerged from Texas. My goodness, I thought to myself, the angels are having a busy week. They keep this up, they'll cover all fifty states from A to Z.

Bingo! There it was! How did I know they hadn't already done that five times over? The results of that sudden enlightenment are what you will find in this book. Where once I had barely enough material to satisfy a high school English teacher's demands for a book report—let alone a book publisher's—suddenly, I found I had too much material.

Now I must ask myself—was it the stories in the paper that enabled me to come up with the idea to do this book—or was there someone else involved, someone looking over my shoulder who wanted these stories told?

What do you think?

The Complete Angel

ENCYCLOPEDIA
of ANGELS

A *through* Z

Abdiel

Mythological angel from the epic poem *Paradise Lost* by John Milton. Abdiel is one of the angels in heaven under the command of the archangel Lucifer. In a plot to overthrow God Lucifer incites the angels under his command to rebellion. He insists that they are destined to rule over heaven, rather than being its mere servants.

Of all the angels assembled before Lucifer, only Abdiel challenges the validity of the archangel's fiery words. He argues that it is insane for a created being to advocate, or attempt, such action against his own maker. How could the creation possibly possess more power than the creator?

Lucifer insists that he is not a created being, but rather an equal with the maker. At this rash statement, Abdiel firmly states that he will have no part in Lucifer's plot and simply flies away. He is the only angel in Lucifer's legions to abandon the archangel. The rest remain with their archangel-leader to face their doom.

Abraham, The angels of

From the Old Testament of the Holy Bible. Abraham was the progenitor and first patriarch of the Hebrew people and the father of Isaac.

According to the Book of Genesis, the Lord witnessed the sin and corruption of the cities of Sodom and Gomorrah and dispatched three angels to destroy the cities and all the people within. Disguised as mortal men, the three angels began their journey to the evil cities. Along the way they stopped at the tent of Abraham. The honorable patriarch provided the three visitors with water for their feet, a place to rest under a shade tree, and a meal of fine meat, cream, and baked bread.

Thus, Abraham found favor in the eyes of the angels to whom he had shown such gracious hospitality, all the while unaware of their holy status.

Abraham had another encounter with an angel in the Book of Genesis in a passage where his faith is sorely tested when God commanded that Abraham sacrifice his only son, Isaac, to show his complete devotion to the Lord. Although he was heartbroken by the command, Abraham's faith was strong. Readying the altar, Abraham prepared Isaac for the sacrifice, but as he was about to drive the knife into the heart of his only son, an angel of the Lord called to Abraham to halt the sacrifice. Abraham won favor in the eyes of the Lord for his unwavering faith and devotion to God's commands.

Af, Angel of Death

From Jewish legend. Af was an angel of death
sent by the archangel Uriel to intercept Moses on
his journey to Egypt. In his haste to fulfill the
Lord's orders to set the Hebrew slaves of Egypt
free, Moses had neglected to perform the act of
circumcision on Gershom, his first born son. This
angered the Lord. Seeing this, Uriel sent forth Af
who quickly swallowed Moses up to his circumcised member. Confusion reigned as Moses tried
to understand this unusual predicament.

It was Zipporah, the wife of Moses, who finally realized the reason for the Lord's displeas-
ure with her husband. Unwrapping the robe
from the baby, Gershom, she quickly circumcised
the child. Cupping a portion of the blood in her
hand, she dripped it at the feet of Moses. Seeing
that the Lord was pleased by this, Uriel ordered
that Af release Moses so that he might continue
his journey to Egypt to free the children of Israel
from the pharaoh.

Angels

Superior spiritual beings, without earthly, material bodies who serve as holy messengers between humans and God in the cosmic order.
They may appear to humans in many different
forms. Often surrounded by brilliant light, they
possess great power and inspire both fear and
awe in those they come in contact with. There
are a number of opinions as to the orders and

rank of angels. The following is the most accepted today, listed in rank from the highest to the lowest:

1. Seraphim
2. Cherubim
3. Thrones
4. Dominions
5. Virtues
6. Powers
7. Princes
8. Archangels
9. Angels

Anpiel

In Jewish religion, mystics of the Kabbalist consider Anpiel the angel who has charge of watching over the birds of the universe.

Apollyon

Often called The Destroyer, Apollyon is found in the Bible's Book of Revelation and is the angel who watches over hell's bottomless pit. It is Apollyon who will chain the powerful Satan and toss him into the bottomless pit where he shall linger one thousand years. At the end of time, the pit will be opened and spew forth swarms of human-faced locusts which will torment sinners for a period of five months. These creatures of torture will be under the control of Apollyon.

Apsaras

Celestial courtesans found in Hindu mythology and in certain Moslem folklore. Among the Hindu these voluptuous nymphs embraced the spirits of the dead as they were carried into the afterlife. Among Moslems it was believed that a soldier who slew a Christian during the period of a Holy War would be rewarded in paradise with two angelic females for his sensual pleasure for eternity.

Armaros

From Jewish legend. The angel Armaros became one of the legions of angels cast out of heaven for fornicating with mortal women and passing on to mankind the forbidden knowledge of casting spells.

Ashmedai

One of the fallen angels of Lucifer's command who, in mythological accounts, oversees hell's casinos. Ashmedai is also credited with influencing Noah's intoxication.

Ashodeus

The demon angel of wanton lust and drunkenness. Apocryphal legend has it that Ashodeus found perverse enjoyment in appearing in bridal chambers and strangling bridegrooms on their wedding nights. On one occasion, Ashodeus eagerly awaited the coming wedding of a widow on whom he had visited this foul practice seven times previously. Having lost seven husbands to this demon angel already, the widow was fearful for the life of her newest love, a young man named Tobais.

Unbeknown to Ashodeus, Tobais had been taken under the protective care of the angel Raphael, the guardian angel of the human race, who is particularly watchful over the young and innocent. On the day Tobais was to be married, the excited youth was on his way to the home of his future bride when he was met on the road by Raphael. The angel warned him of Ashodeus and the demon's plans for the boy.

Understandably shaken by this news, young Tobais asked, "What can I hope to do against a demon angel?"

Raphael told him first to get a fish. He was then to gut the fish and remove the liver, heart, and gall. That night, before going to bed with his bride, he was to place the organs in the fireplace of the bridal chamber.

That night, Tobais did as he had been instructed. When Ashodeus appeared in the bedroom, he was ill prepared for the foul odor of the smoke and the crackling sound of the smoldering, greasy organs that greeted him. Unable to withstand the stench, the demon angel flew from the bridal chamber, traveling as far as Egypt in order to rid himself of the foul smell. It was while in Egypt that Ashodeus encountered an angel of the Lord. In a struggle between good and evil, Ashodeus was subdued, tied up, and cast back into hell by the Lord's angel.

Azazel

From folklore. Azazel was one of two hundred angels who, after seeing the beauty of mortal women, descended from heaven to engage in sex with the women of the earth. Because of this unbridled lustfulness, all two hundred fell from grace in the eyes of the Lord and were cast out of heaven.

Azazel brought further wrath upon himself, as did others with him, by teaching humans the forbidden knowledge of weapon-making, how to write, and vanity. Among Hebrew mystics, Azazel had not always been a fallen angel, but rather, a desert creature of the Old Testament who each year served the Hebrew high priest.

On the Hebrew Day of Atonement, the priest brought forth a goat upon which all the sins committed by Israel during the year were symbolically loaded. This goat was driven out into the desert for the pleasure of Azazel—thereby cleansing and purifying the children of Israel of all sins committed that year. In later years, after further study, the mystics themselves deemed Azazel a fallen angel.

Azrael

The Islamic Angel of Death. The servant of Allah, Azrael has four faces covered with a million veils which conceal a body completely covered with eyes. Each eye symbolizing a living being. Each blink of an eye signifies a dying mortal somewhere in the world.

Azrael moves about on four large wings and carries a book which lists the names of all living humans upon the earth. Below the throne of Allah stands a great tree with leaves bearing the name of each and every living being upon the earth. The dropping of one of these leaves from the tree signifies that the time ordered by Allah for that person to die has come. Azrael, the angel of death, bears up the fallen leaf, reads the name, and after a period of forty days, proceeds to separate the soul from the chosen person's body and to send it on its way to paradise.

Balberith

A fallen angel who, according to medieval occultists, serves as hell's secretary and archivist. Chief among his duties is the notarizing of deals made between mortals and the Devil.

Bardiel

From the Ethiopic Book of Enoch. The angel of lightning.

Beelzebub

Originally, a Philistine deity. The name means "lord of the flies." In the New Testament, Beelzebub is referred to as the prince of demons. Legend and Milton's *Paradise Lost* often refer to him as Satan's foremost lieutenant. In a tale from ancient folklore, Beelzebub and Satan have a direct confrontation with Christ in the tomb following the crucifixion. Mythology has it that during the three days before the Resurrection, Christ stormed the gates of hell showing the two powerful demons his invincibility by facing the test of Satan's most intense hellfire and emerging unscathed.

During his time in Satan's domain, Christ released certain virtuous pagans from bondage. Among these were John the Baptist, King David, and the prophet Isaiah.

According to the Gospel of Nicodemus, Beelzebub, having seen the power of Christ, avidly ridiculed Satan's ignorance for having engineered the crucifixion of Christ on earth. In his defense, Satan claimed that he had done so in the belief that at Christ's death, the son of God would become his prisoner in hell forever. Satan had to admit that he had sorely underestimated the power of Christ.

Belial

From the epic poem *Paradise Lost*. The demon angel of lewdness and reasonable sounding lies. In mythology, hell's ambassador to Turkey.

Belphegor

Demon angel of inventiveness. Middle Age occult mythology considered Belphegor hell's ambassador to France, specifically to the less than moral city of Paris. According to legend, it was Belphegor who was sent up to the surface of the earth to investigate rumors in hell that there were some happily married couples in God's creation. Upon his return, Belphegor informed his master, Satan, that from all he had seen and heard transpire between all the married couples of the earth there was no truth to the rumors.

Bethelda

The angel identified by the famed theosophical clairvoyant Geoffrey Hodson. By Hodson's own account, an angel made contact with him and identified itself as the angel Bethelda. This angel proceeded to assist Hodson, through visual revelations, in the writing of five books. Among these, a book entitled *The Brotherhood of Angels and Men*, published in 1927.

Chamuel

The angel Chamuel is believed by various groups to be the Dark Angel who wrestled with Jacob in the Book of Genesis. He is also believed to be the angel who comforted Jesus in the Garden of Gethsemane following Jesus' betrayal by Judas and remained with the son of God until the soldiers arrived to arrest him.

Cherubim

Second in rank of the nine Orders of Angels. Often referred to as God's record keepers as well as the guardians of the light and of the stars.

Cherubim is plural form of cherub. The basic appearance of the cherub is a winged sphinx, or winged lion with a human head. A pair of cherubim of colossal size overshadowed the ark of Salomon's temple. The modern concept of a cherub as a small, winged boy came about from the traditions of Renaissance artists.

In the Book of Genesis, cherubim were placed at the entrance to the Garden of Eden to protect the tree of life and to guard against the return of Adam and Eve who had been banished from the garden for picking fruit from the tree of knowledge.

Dark Angel

From the Bible Book of Genesis. He is the angel (some claim this was the angel Chamuel) whom Jacob encountered on the shores of the River Jabbok. The mortal and the angel wrestled through the predawn hours. Struggle as he might, the angel found he could not get the better of Jacob. Seeing that dawn was fast approaching, the angel resorted to his holy power and, touching Jacob's hip, he cast it out of joint. Desperate to leave before a new day broke, the angel tried to flee but Jacob refused to relinquish his grip upon the angel until the dark angel agreed to bless him.

The angel agreed, then, after blessing Jacob, he also gave him a new name. This can be found in Genesis 32:28: " . . . Thy name shall be called no more Jacob, but Israel: for as a prince hast thou power with God and with men, and hast prevailed."

Devils

Chief and leader of these demons is the fallen archangel Lucifer. According to many religions, the Devil is an evil spirit that opposes God. Devils tempt people to become wicked. In Judaism and Christianity, the Devil is also known as Satan. In Islam, the religion of the Muslims, the Devil is called Iblis.

The Christian religion teaches that devils are the fallen angels who foolishly followed the archangel Lucifer in his rebellion against God which resulted in Lucifer and all of his followers being expelled from heaven.

Many Christians believe that the Devil now rules over hell where he and his fallen followers render punishment unto the damned and continuously tempt humanity to turn against God.

Djibril

From Islam. Djibril is the Moslem equivalent of the archangel Gabriel. It was Djibril who appeared to the prophet Mohammed and dictated to him the holy words of the Koran. Once this work was completed, Djibril took Mohammed to the Dome of the Rock, one of Islam's holiest shrines. From here, Mohammed climbed a golden ladder to the heavens where he encountered Jesus, Moses, Abraham, the archangel Michael, and Adam, the first man. Directed by Djibril to enter into a golden light, Mohammed received knowledge of the divine. He was then returned to earth.

In Moslem folklore it was Djibril who gave comfort to Adam following man's expulsion from the Garden of Eden.

Dominions

Fourth in rank of the nine Orders of the Angels. Dominions are the heavenly order which governs the activities of all angelic groups that are of lower status than themselves. Its members are divine bureaucrats who decide what needs to be done to accomplish God's infinite goals.

Dubbiel

Angel of Jewish legend. Dubbiel was the established guardian angel of the great Persian Empire.

Ezekeel

From ancient Jewish legend. The corruption of the human race was hastened by the fallen angels of heaven who had fornicated with mortal women and passed on to mankind forbidden knowledge. It was the fallen angel Ezekeel who taught the humans how to tell the future by watching the clouds.

Gabriel

A prominent angel in several Biblical narratives. The name means "God is our strength." There are many events and predictions accredited to the angel Gabriel. Often referred to as God's messenger, Gabriel assisted Daniel in the interpetation of visions and the making of predictions. He was the angel who came to Mary and revealed to her the importance of the son she was to bear. He foretold to Mary's cousin, Elizabeth, that she would be the mother of John the Baptist.

It is believed in the Moslem faith that Gabriel dictated the Koran to the prophet Mohammed. In Jewish legend, the angel Gabriel parted the Red Sea to allow Moses and the children of Israel to escape the wrath of the pharaoh's soldiers.

In Christianity, Gabriel will appear at the end of time and blow the last trumpet call announcing the coming of the final judgment.

In Milton's *Paradise Lost*, Gabriel commands the angels guarding the Garden of Eden from Satan in the hope of protecting God's creations, Adam and Eve, from the vengeful retribution of the archangel Lucifer, who had been expelled from heaven.

Other titles often attributed to Gabriel include Heaven's Treasurer, Chief Ambassador to Humanity, and Interpreter of Dreams and Visions.

Hadarniel

From Louis Ginsberg's *The Legends of the Jews*. A massive, towering angel who is the gatekeeper to heaven. Hadarniel confronted Moses when the leader of the children of Israel arrived in heaven to secure the Bible's first five books, containing the Laws of Moses. Unaware that God had authorized Moses to remove the books, Hadarniel denied the leader entrance into heaven and threatened Moses with such force that Moses became afraid and began to weep. God intervened and after scolding Hadarniel, God made him serve as Moses' guide, whereupon Hadarniel led Moses to the holy books and assured the leader's safe return back to earth.

Hafaza

Moslem legend refers to the Hafaza as guardian angels. Each person has assigned four Hafaza to guard against evil spirits. The four share the duties of protecting their ward, two by day and two by night. They also maintain a record book of their ward's deeds, both good and bad. This book will be presented as evidence of a person's life on earth at Judgment Day. According to legend the most dangerous time for a mortal is at dawn or at twilight, the times when the guardian angels are changing shifts. It is at these times that the evil spirits are the strongest and seek to influence humans to do evil.

Harut

A fallen angel from Moslem legend. Shortly after the beginning of time, Harut went to Mohammed and spoke of the evil lust, sin, and decay of morals among the people of the earth. Allah agreed with Harut but retorted that he, Harut, could not have done any better had he been in the hapless mortals' place. Harut quickly argued that this was not so, and to prove it presented Allah with a challenge. Harut and another angel would descend to earth and move among the mortals and do so without becoming corrupt as the humans were. Allah agreed, but warned that there were a number of mortal sins which they must protect themselves from—chief among them—

the worshipping of false gods, womanizing, murder, and the drinking of wine or spirits.

Harut and his companion, an angel named Marut, agreed. However, they were not among the mortals long before they came upon a mortal woman of exceptional beauty and were both overcome with desire to have her. She refused their advances and would only yield if they committed the very sins which Allah had warned them against. Both chose the least of the four sins and drank wine, but they quickly became intoxicated. While in a drunken state they killed a man who had come upon them and witnessed their condition. At the sight of the murder, the woman uttered the name of Allah which Harut had told her about while drinking. At the sound of the name, she was lifted up to heaven where she became the star Venus. When Harut and Marut regained their senses they found that, for their sins, they had lost the power of their wings and could never again return to heaven.

Hayy

The Wandering Angel found in Moslem religion, who tutored the renowned philosopher and thinker Avicenna concerning the mysteries of the universe. Avicenna had always been puzzled by the perplexing ways of the Earth's mortals and asked Hayy to explain that great mystery to him. Hayy answered that humans were a hybrid of two natures—on the one side was the Spirit, which maintained a reverence toward God and his teaching, and on the other side, the Soul, which was all too easily given over to evil and mischievous ways.

Houris

From Moslem folklore. Houris are the angel-like women of uncommon beauty, with coal black eyes and silken voices who exist in paradise. According to legend, when a Moslem male dies his soul is delivered up to paradise. Upon entering this holy place each man is provided with seventy-two Houris. Their sole purpose is to provide sexual pleasure to the assigned new arrival. Following a sexual encounter, each Houris' virginity is totally restored.

Iblis

From the Moslem holy book of the Koran. The name is derived from the Greek word *diabolos*, and is the Moslem equal to the Christian term devil. In the beginning Iblis was God's administrator over the earth and the lower heavens. According to the Koran, when Allah created the first man, Adam, He ordered the angels of paradise to bow down before his creation. Iblis alone refused. Protesting vehemently to Allah, Iblis argued that he was better than Adam, for Allah had made Iblis and all the other angels from fire, while Adam had been made from mere mud. For

this rebelling against Allah, Iblis was damned
and cast from paradise.

In revenge for this, Iblis, through deceit and
deception, tricked Hawwa (Eve) into eating the
forbidden fruit from the tree of evil. When Allah
discovered what she had done, He punished her
with menstruation, pregnancy, and the pains of
childbirth. Eventually both she and Adam were
cast from paradise.

Iniaes

One of seven angels denounced by Pope Za-
chary and a church council in 745 A.D. in an effort to quelch the ever growing list of named
angels that existed at that time. In a sweeping
change, the council declared that no angels
would be called upon for help, except for the
three mentioned in the Bible (Michael, Raphael,
and Gabriel).

According to mythology, Iniaes was outraged,
for when Lucifer had rebelled against God, Iniaes had stood firmly by the Lord. Now, his
name was being wiped from existence. Unable to
control his anger, Iniaes departed from heaven
and joined the ranks of the fallen angels. In revenge, Iniaes delights in breaking wind whenever an overly pompous preacher makes a deep
remark.

Isa

From Moslem religion. The name is a variation
of Jesus. To the Moslem, Isa is high among the
heavenly occupants closest to Allah.

Allah observed Isa on earth where he worked
miracles, healed the sick, and resurrected the
dead. Seeing that Isa was about to be taken by
armed men who feared his powers, Allah caused
another man to take on Isa's appearance and this
man was arrested and crucified in Isa's place. For
his unselfish deeds upon the Earth, Allah took
Isa up into paradise where he would be pro-
tected for all time.

Israfil

The Islamic angel of Judgment Day. Israfil is
the equivalent of the Christian angel Gabriel. It
is Israfil who shall stand upon the Holy Rock in
Jerusalem on Judgment Day and sound the final
trumpet that shall mark the coming of God.

It is said that Israfil gazes down into hell six
times a day and is so overcome by the suffering
he sees that Allah must continuously stop Israfil's flowing tears from flooding the Earth. Israfil
is also the Islamic angel of music. One story
states that Allah uses the sweet breath of Israfil
to spawn forth thousands of angels to sing the
praises of the Almighty.

Ithuriel

Mythological angel from Milton's *Paradise Lost*. Learning that Satan has invaded the Garden of Eden, and fearful for the safety of Adam and Eve, the archangel Gabriel sends forth a search party of angels to search out the ruler of hell and to chase him from the garden.

Ithuriel is one of two angels who discovers Satan in the garden. Satan is disguised as a toad, and hiding near the head of Eve. When discovered by Ithuriel, the demon is whispering temptations into the ear of the sleeping woman. Ithuriel reaches out and touches the prince of darkness with his spear. Satan is instantly transformed into his true form, a hideous creature, and flees the garden, but his evil words have already planted the seeds of temptation in Eve's mind. This temptation later leads to Adam and Eve's expulsion from the Garden of Eden.

Jaoel

From Jewish religion. Jaoel is heaven's choir director. Jaoel once escorted the Jewish patriarch Abraham on a visit to heaven. Once there, Abraham began to ask such thought-provoking questions of Jaoel that the angel had to direct the Jewish leader to God himself.

Joel

Angel from the *Book of Adam and Eve*. Pleased with his creation of the first man and woman, the Lord sent forth the angel Joel with instructions for Adam. The message carried by Joel made Adam responsible for naming all the creatures of the new world.

Jophiel

Believed by many to be the guardian angel of the tree of knowledge in the Garden of Eden. Symbolized by the flaming sword, the angel Jophiel drove Adam and Eve from the Garden. Jophiel also served as the guardian angel of the three sons of Noah.

Kakabel

A controversial angel who has been deemed a good angel by some and a fallen angel by others. On the one side he is acknowledged as the overseer of the stars and constellations, an exalted and powerful angel, forever loyal to his creator. On the other side, there is a group that have named Kakabel as one of the fallen angels cast from heaven for lusting after mortal women, and who compounded his troubles by teaching mankind the mysteries of the stars and the study of astrology.

Kemuel

From Jewish folklore. Kemuel is the Gatekeeper of Heaven, named in *The Legend of the Jews, Volume III* by Louis Ginsberg. Kemuel and his staff of twelve thousand angels refused to allow Moses entry through the gates of heaven to retrieve the Torah for the wandering Jews during their forty years in the wilderness. Moses attempted to explain his mission a second time, but Kemuel again refused him entry. Knowing of his people's suffering in the wilderness and their need for the Torah, Moses became outraged and struck the angel with such a powerful blow that Moses "destroyed Kemuel out of this world."

Lahash

From Jewish legend. Lahash, a good natured, but not exceptionally bright angel, teamed up with another angel to intercept a prayer from Moses, in which the Jewish leader prayed for answers concerning death. Not wanting to burden the Lord with such a disheartening prayer, Lahash and his fellow angel, Zakum, rallied over a million spirits to halt the prayer from reaching God's ears, but they were caught. For their attempted disruption of Moses' prayer, each angel was punished with sixty fiery lashes of a whip.

Lailah

From Jewish folklore, the angel of conception, often referred to as "The angel of the night." According to legend, when a woman conceives it is the angel Lailah who carries the sperm to a holy place before the throne of God. Here, the Lord makes his decision as to what kind of child shall be born, boy or girl, rich or poor, beautiful or ugly.

Malik

From Moslem religion. Malik is the rightful angel-overseer of hell, not Iblis (Satan). There are nineteen angels who serve as Malik's guards over hell's boundaries. Malik's hell contains both Moslems and infidels alike. Malik is a hard taskmaster, stirring the fires of hell often to hear the cries of the sinners in his charge.

Mammon

The fallen angel of greed. In English, the word Mammon has become a personification of money as a false God for the greedy. The angel Mammon appears in Milton's *Paradise Lost*, where he has a habit of staring constantly down at the golden walkways of heaven, rather than at his creator. The word mammon can be found in the Gospels, where Jesus states: "No man can be a slave to two masters; you cannot serve both God and Mammon."

Mefathiel

From Jewish folklore, the guardian angel of thieves. Although they were clearly in violation of one of the Ten Commandments, the angel Mefathiel took pity upon the less fortunate whose only means of survival was stealing from the more well-to-do. Mefathiel would plead the case of the poor thief before the bookkeepers of life, as long as the act was one of survival for oneself or family, but quickly disavow and condemn the thief who stole for the purpose of greed.

Mehiel

From Kabbalist mystics. Mehiel is the guardian angel of writers and teachers who oversees the protection of the scholars and often bestows the gift of patience and direction for increased knowledge and understanding.

Mephistopheles

From medieval mythology. Mephistopheles is a fallen archangel, a master of persuasion and etiquette. In some tales he is an agent of Lucifer, in others, the Prince of Darkness himself. Mostly famous for his role in the poetic play *Faust* by Goethe, wherein a man signs a contract in blood with Mephistopheles. The man receives power, position, and riches—in return, Mephistopheles receives the man's soul.

Metatron

The throne angel, heaven's secretary who records the minutes of all celestial and earthy occurrences for safe keeping in God's archives. In Jewish folklore, Metatron is one of heaven's greatest angels. Sitting beside God, Metatron records all of the good and bad deeds of Israel. It is believed that Metatron, the Cherubim and the Seraphim are the only angels in all of heaven who are allowed in God's most holy throne room.

Michael

One of only three named angels in Scripture, the others being Gabriel and Raphael. Michael's name is a question meaning Who is God? Best known of the archangels, Michael is acknowledged by all three major western sacred traditions. Believed to be the first and most powerful of God's created beings, he is God's soldier-general and protector of righteousness, therefore the most powerful angel in heaven.

Among the many feats and titles attributed to this mighty angel are the defeat of Lucifer and his rebellious angels during the War in Heaven, a war in which Lucifer attempted to overthrow God and become the ruler of all creation. He appeared to Moses as the fire in the burning bush and rescued Daniel and his friends from the lion's den. He is reported to be the angel who appeared to Mary and told her of her approaching death, assuring her that there was nothing to fear, for he himself would escort her to heaven when the end came. Michael is also purported to be the angel in charge of guiding the souls of the newly dead into the afterlife. He is said to be the angel of the Last Judgment, where he will weigh the souls of all to determine their final fate.

When tried as a witch by the English, Joan of Arc identified the angel Michael as one of those that had empowered her to drive the English from France during the Hundred Years War. In 1950, Pope Pius XII declared the angel Michael as the patron angel of police officers.

In the mythology of the Book of Adam and Eve, when God gathered all the angels of heaven together and presented his human creation, the first man, Adam, to them, God commanded them to bow down before the first man as a sign of respectful homage. Michael, to show his total obedience to God and to set the example, was the first to bow down before Adam.

Mikal

From Moslem religion. Mikal is the equivalent of the Christian archangel Michael. He reigns in the seventh heaven. According to Moslem folklore, Mikal has not laughed since the creation of hell. Mikal has emerald wings and a coat of saffron hair. Each hair contains a million faces, each face a million eyes and a million tongues, each speaking a million languages—all of which beg Allah's forgiveness.

Minos

From Dante's *Divine Comedy*. Minos is the fallen angel appointed Satan's judge at the gates of hell. Upon arrival at Satan's fiery domain, the unfortunate stand before Minos and await the judging angel's assignment of their souls to a particular place of torment within the confines of Hell.

Mithra

From the Zoroastrian religion of ancient Persia, a word meaning friend. Mithra was the leader of the Yazatas—the good spirits—and second in command, exceeded only by Ahura Mazda (God). Mithra was charged with the awesome job of holding the world together during the cosmic war between Ahura Mazda and the Ahriman (The Evil)—a forerunner of Satan or the Devil. In the period of the Roman Empire, Mithra lost his angel status among the Roman legions. The soldiers preferred to bestow a new title upon Mithra, calling him Mithras—the Sun God. It was believed among the Roman military that Mithras granted them life after death. Soon the belief in Mithras became so strong that it evolved into its own religion—Mithraism.

Mithraism held striking similarities to early Christianity, stressing the importance of brotherly love, humility, communion, baptism, life after death, and a final judgment day. The major difference between the two religions however, proved to be the turning point that sent Mithraism into obscurity and Christianity on to what we know it as today—that difference was Mithraism's tolerance for the worship of other gods.

Nasargiel

From Jewish religion. The angel Nasargiel was chosen to serve as a guide for Moses, who had requested of the Lord a tour of hell so as to better enlighten his people on the woes of a sinful life and the terrible fate that would await them should they fall from grace in the eyes of God. One of the many sights that Moses observed on his tour were men hanging by their eyelids from a line. Moses asked Nasargiel the purpose of this unusual torture and what the poor souls had done to warrant such treatment. Nasargiel answered that these were men who had looked lustfully and with sin in their hearts upon the wives of their neighbors while living upon the Earth.

Nisroc

From medieval folklore. Once an angel of prominence, Nisroc had at various times stood guard over the forbidden tree of knowledge in the Garden of Eden, an honorable task among God's most trusted angels. Nisroc unfortunately came under the influence of the archangel Lucifer and joined with his legion in Lucifer's attempted overthrow of God. For this, Nisroc was cast from heaven along with Lucifer and his host of rebel angels. Nisroc is now said to serve as hell's dietician and the head chef of hell's most damning recipes.

Pahaliah

Of Jewish origin. Pahaliah is the angel ancient Jewish Kabbalists would call upon when they would encounter disbelievers. Through the power of Pahaliah the Kabbalists sought to convert such disbelievers to the ways of God.

Penemue

From the ancient Ethiopic Book of Enoch. It was the fallen angel Penemue who taught mankind the forbidden knowledge of writing, and later drew the wrath of Noah who stated that it was through Penemue's forbidden teachings that many mortals became sinners from eternity to this very day.

Pen-Ming

Of Chinese origin, Taoist religion. Pen-Ming is the guardian spirit of ordained Masters of Taoism and serves as a messenger between the masters and the rulers of the universe.

Powers

Ranked sixth in the nine Orders of the Angels, powers maintain the delicate balance of God's created universe.

Princes

Ranked seventh in the nine Orders of the Angels, princes are charged with the responsibility of standing guard over nations and their leaders. They possess the power to govern the rise and fall of their respective nations and to protect the good from the evil onslaught of jealous spirits.

Raguel

The angel charged with the responsibility of overseeing the behavior of all of heaven's angels and assuring that they keep God's commands and remain vigilant against Lucifer's ever-present temptations which can lead to an angel's corruption and banishment from heaven.

Rahtiel

From the Book of Enoch. Possessing an eye for things of great beauty, the angel Rahtiel was chosen to be the angel in charge of the constellations in God's creation. Rahtiel oversees the death and creation of new stars and systems throughout the universe and assures that balance is maintained within the galaxy.

Ramiel

From the book of Enoch, the angel of thunder. Ramiel's clapping of his hands is said to cause the thunder we hear in thunderstorms. The clapping comes from his joy of seeing the Earth cleansed by the rains of the angel Matriel and dried by the winds of the angel Ruhiel.

Raphael

Considered by many to be the most endearing of God's angels, Raphael is deemed the guardian angel of the human race. His name means "God Has Healed." Raphael is particularly fond of young people. Serving as supervisor of all guardian angels, Raphael oversees their actions. He himself specializes in healing and nurturing creativity. He healed the pain of circumcision for Abraham, who had the procedure performed at an advanced age. Raphael also ministered to Jacob who had been injured wrestling the angel Chamuel. Raphael takes special interest in those who seek spiritual growth and awareness in their lives. Raphael is often depicted as a traveler, carrying a walking stick and a gourd containing water slung over his shoulder as he wanders the earth in search of those seeking spiritual guidance and knowledge of God.

Rashiel

From the Book of Enoch. The angel of cyclones and tornadoes, Rashiel is known for his creativity and often careless use of the Earth's environment. He found that he could create a whirling motion upon the land or in the water by merely moving his finger in a circle. Delighted at this, he often entertained himself by creating these whirlwinds of destruction until one day he was scolded by God. However, like a bad boy scolded by a teacher, he ignores the warning and occasionally joins with his fellow angels, Ruhiel, the Angel of Wind and Matriel, the Angel of Rain, to create storms upon the Earth.

Rashnu

From Zoroastrian religion. Rashnu is the judge of souls seeking entrance into heaven. In Christian belief, the soul seeks entrance at the gates of heaven; however, in Zoroastrian religion, the soul of the deceased must cross the Cinvat Bridge, the link between earth and heaven. The guardian of this bridge is the angel Rashnu. A stern overseer, Rashnu makes the soul wait for three days while he reviews the records in the book of life in which are recorded the good deeds, as well as the bad deeds, performed by the new arrival during his time upon the earth. The deeds are weighted against each other on a set of golden scales. Once judged, the worthy soul is assisted across the difficult crossing by a maiden of heavenly beauty. For the wicked soul, attempting to cross the bridge proves impossible. The bridge narrows to a razor's edge and the wicked quickly lose their balance and fall into the blackness below, where wait the devils and demons that delight in tormenting the wicked souls for all eternity.

Raziel

From Jewish folklore. The angel Raziel is purported to be the all seeing and hearing angel who stands behind the curtains that are drawn around the throne of God. It was the angel Raziel who took pity upon Adam and Eve following their expulsion from the Garden of Eden. Aware of the difficulties that faced the lost couple due to their lack of knowledge, Raziel presented Adam with *The Book of the Angel Raziel*. This book contained all the knowledge of the universe. It was through this book that Adam and Eve survived their early days out of the Garden of Eden.

Remiel

From Jewish folklore. Found in the Book of Enoch, Remiel is an angel of controversy. He can be found listed as one of the heavenly archangels, which would place him in the company of other angels such as the powerful Gabriel and Michael, and one of the seven permitted to stand in the presence of God. Yet, in the same book, he is later found listed as one of the fallen angels. No explanation is given.

Ridwan

Origin is in Islam. The angel Ridwan is the Moslem guardian of the entrance into Paradise (Heaven). Passage is granted past this awesome angel guardian only after a thorough examination of the books in which are kept a daily record of the new arrival's good and evil deeds while on earth. Once Ridwan has evaluated the recorded deeds, he will either grant passage into paradise or brutally cast the unholy soul headlong into the pit of darkness below, where evil demons shall administer a host of tortures upon the soul until the end of time.

Ruhiel

From the Book of Enoch. The angel of wind, Ruhiel is charged with providing a cooling breeze over the surface of the earth. He was considered a God in his own right by early sailors and seamen. Sometimes influenced by the horseplay of the angel Rashiel, Ruhiel allows his powers to exceed the norm and his winds to be utilized in the cyclones and tornadoes created by the playful Rashiel.

Samael

Recognized in both Christian and Jewish religion. Here we find another angel who is considered both a good angel and a bad angel. Often referred to as the angel of death, it was Samael who supposedly brought mortality into the world. Jewish legend contends that when it came time for Moses to die, God ordered his mighty angel Gabriel to go forth upon the earth and carry the soul of the great Jewish leader up to heaven. Gabriel humbly requested that he be excused from this task. The angel Michael also asked to be excused from this sad duty. Neither wanted the loved and righteous Moses to taste death at his hand.

Aware of the great love his most trusted archangels held for this great leader, God granted their requests. He then turned to Samael, the angel of death. Not one known for his sentimentality, Samael happily accepted the task and with sword in hand swooped down from heaven to confront the spiritual giant of the Jews. But when this hardened angel stepped before Moses, the holy leader's face shone with such a brilliant radiance that Samael became afraid and he fled back to heaven without the soul of Moses.

God was beside himself with anger at Samael and ordered that the Angel of Death go back down and complete his assigned task. This confrontation did not go well for Samael, for Moses, knowing the angel's purpose, attacked the angel with his legendary staff and blinded Samael. At

this point, God himself intervened and ordered
Gabriel, Michael, and Moses' teacher and men-
tor, the angel Zagzagel, to carry Moses' soul to
heaven on a couch. Moses finally gave in to
God's will, but halfway to heaven Moses' soul
again objected and began to fight with the angels. God then intervened and kissed Moses. The
patriarch's soul joyfully leaped from the elderly
leader's body and continued the journey without
further incident. Realizing clearly the hardship of
the task he had placed upon Samael, God restored the angel's sight and heralded the courage
of his Angel of Death.

There is a second legend that demonstrates the
dark side of this angel. Following Adam and
Eve's expulsion from the Garden of Eden, the
couple lost their immortality and had no idea of
what they would do or how to maintain their
progress of the human race. Seeing this, Samael
gathered around him a group of tempting angels
and disguising themselves as men and women
in the likeness of Adam and Eve, put on a
shameless sexual exhibition before the confused
couple. Adam, unsure of what he saw happening
before him called upon God for guidance. Dis-
covering Samael's deed, God thwarted the possible sinning of Adam and Eve by marrying the
couple.

Sariel

From the Book of Enoch. Sariel is one of the
archangels responsible for determining the des-

tiny of fellow angels who have willingly and knowingly flouted God's laws.

Satan

Referred to as Lucifer or the Devil. This fallen angel is the epitome of pure evil within the Christian religion.

This, however, was not always the case. At one time the angel Lucifer was the greatest and most highly honored of all angels created by God. Lucifer's beauty and superior intelligence was unequaled by his peers. Many Christians believe that it was those very things which led to this angel's tragic downfall. Some contend that it was conceit and jealous envy that led to the great angel's rebellion against his creator. Others declare that it was arrogance that provided the spark that ignited the War in Heaven and eventually led to the defeat of Lucifer and his band of rebellious angels—a fate which resulted in their being cast from heaven forever.

Satan is visualized by many religions in many ways. Medieval priests saw him as a figure adorned with horns, a face behind him, cloven feet, and a hairy body emitting an odor so foul that it could not be described. Others see him as a hideous figure with horns, coal-black, dead eyes, a tail, and razor sharp claws. In Dante's *Divine Comedy*, Satan is pictured as a giant with bat's wings buried in a lake of ice. He is described chewing on the bodies of the world's three greatest sinners known to Dante, the slayers of Julius Casear, Brutus and Cassius, and the betrayer of Jesus—Judas Iscariot.

It is believed that Satan can alter his appearance at will. He may appear an innocent child, an attractive maiden, even as an angel. His primary purpose is the temptation of mankind, for only by competing for the souls of mankind can he continue his battle with God. Each soul that he manages to steal away from the Lord makes Satan rejoice and serves to fire his spiteful revenge against God for having expelled him and his followers from heaven. Satan's most valuable weapons of temptation are money, power, and sexual lust—all these vices top the list of mankind's most sought after objectives. It is said that more than one human has forfeited or been willing to forfeit his or her very soul for any one of these temptations offered to them by Satan.

Semjaza

From the Book of Enoch. Semjaza was so taken by the beauty of mortal women upon the earth that he became sexually obsessed with mating with them. Convincing two hundred of his fellow angels that they could secretly journey to earth and have as many of these maidens as they wanted without God finding out, he led the group down to earth to begin their orgy of lust. They were wrong. God did find out and the source of his rage was two fold. One, they had attempted to deceive their creator while indulging in their illicit sexual activity with mortal women which they all knew was a great sin in God's eyes. Second, and what God considered an even greater sin, they had taught the mortals forbidden and harmful knowledge that could only lead to further corruption of the children of the Earth.

For their dishonesty and violation of God's orders, Semjaza and all two hundred followers were cast out of heaven and imprisoned in the earth's valleys where they will remain until doomsday and the final judgment.

Seraphim

Ranked first in the nine Orders of the Angels, the seraphim are closest to God and were created with the perfect and total understanding of the creator and are therefore aflame with their love of God. The name means "the burning ones." They represent total peace, contemplation, and perennial love.

Shamshiel

From Hebrew myth. He was the angel prince of the Garden of Eden. When Moses requested a tour of heaven, God granted the patriarch's request. During the tour, Moses was taken to the gates of the Garden of Eden, where Shamshiel met him and served as his guide through the garden. Among the many sights pointed out by Shamshiel was a circle of seventy jeweled thrones upon which sit the most righteous, among them Noah and Abraham.

Srassha

From Zoroastrian religion. He is the all-hearing angel who monitors the complaints and pleas of earthly mortals tormented or wronged by evil-doers. Srassha's busiest hours are at night, the evil-doers preferring the darkness in which to work their mischief. This is also the time when Srassha personally appears on earth and pursues Aesthma, the evil demon of violence and anger. For his devotion to duty, he is only one of a limited number who are allowed to stand in the presence of Ahura Mazda (God).

Suiel

From the Book of Enoch. Suiel is the angel of earthquakes. This angel earned his title through his rambunctious battles with those fallen angels who often attempt to escape from the fiery furnaces of hell. Ever watchful, Suiel is quick to openly challenge any attempted escapee and delights in doing battle. Foregoing weapons, this angel takes on his challengers bare-handed with a series of wrestling moves and body slams that shake the earth itself. Always victorious, Suiel casts the escapee back into the pit and reassumes his watchful perch overlooking the pit.

Thrones

Ranked third in the nine Orders of the Angels, the Thrones serve as a court to consider the disposition of God's decisions.

Tsadkiel

From Jewish folklore. The angel Tsadkiel has a variety of titles and duties in heaven—chief among these is his position as heaven's supply officer. It is this angel's responsibility to issue newly arriving souls their white robes and sandals. His overall title is the angel of justice. He governs the planet Jupiter and at one time was charged with the duty of protecting the patriarch Abraham.

Uriel

Recognized by both the Christian and Jewish religions. There are two interpretations of the name—"God's Light" and "Fire of God." Ranked as a seraph, and overseer of Hades, Uriel is best known as the Archangel of Salvation. Symbolized by a book and a scroll, this angel of prophecy and interpretation takes a particular interest in writers and teachers. Although not as well known as his fellow angels, Gabriel and Michael, Uriel has held many important positions and duties, chief among these was serving as the spirit with the fiery sword who stood at the gates of the lost Eden and as the messenger sent to warn Noah of the coming flood that would destroy the earth.

Uzza

From Jewish folklore. He was one of the angels assigned to watch over a nation. Uzza competed with the angel Rahab for the right to serve as the guardian angel over the nation of Egypt, a position many angels considered one of dishonor, given the Egyptian treatment of the children of Israel.

Virtues

Ranked fifth in the nine Orders of the Angels, they are the workers of miracles granted by God for use on earth. The Virtues also provide courage to those who perform deeds of nobility and virtue against all things evil.

Vohu Manah

From Zoroastrian Religion. He is the archangel believed to be responsible for the initiation of the religion of Zoroastrianism, a religion that eventually brought about radical changes to Judaism and Christian beliefs and doctrine. Zoroastrianism came about around 600 B.C. when the Persian prophet Zoroaster was visited by the archangel Vohu Manah, who bestowed upon the prophet God's words and teachings. Zoroaster in turn formed the Zoroastrian religion which soon swept the ancient Persian Empire and spread to points beyond.

Wormwood

From the Book of Revelation in the Christian Bible. This angel is not directly referred to by name, but rather by the term "star". Wormwood will play a part in the final days of the Earth before the great coming of God, appearing, after the opening of the seventh seal, as a giant flaming star which will streak to earth, striking one-third of the Earth's rivers, creeks, and springs. The waterways will become instantly poisoned by Wormwood's touch and cause the death and suffering of countless mortals in the final days.

Zadkiel

From Jewish legend. Symbolized by the sacrificial knife, Zadkiel is credited with stopping the hand of the prophet Abraham from slaying his son as a sacrifice in a test of the prophet's undying faith in God. There are those who do not agree with this theory—preferring to credit the angel Michael with this act.

Zafiel

From the ancient Ethiopic Book of Enoch. Zafiel is referred to as the Angel of Showers. Legend has it that this angel acquired this position due to the highly emotional feelings that swept over him whenever he looked down upon the earth. If he saw suffering, whether in man or beast, Zafiel could not help but weep, his tears falling to earth in the form of rainshowers.

Zagzagel

From Jewish legend. This angel was chosen by God to serve as a tutor to the great leader, Moses. Zagzagel guided Moses through the workings of miracles before the pharaoh and his court in Egypt. Zagzagel was always available to Moses to answer the often confusing questions the leader of the children of Israel had regarding certain events and happenings that occurred as they were led from Egypt and toward the promised land. Zagzagel was also one of the angels God called upon to assist the archangels Michael and Gabriel when it came time for Moses to die and his soul to be carried up to heaven.

Zakkiel

From the Book of Enoch. Zakkiel is the Enochian angel of storms. A warrior-angel in the great battle of heaven, Zakkiel did not agree with the mere banishment of the rebellious angels and thought their punishment should have been far more severe. His view, however, was not shared by the creator. Zakkiel reluctantly accepted this state of affairs, but still rants and raves about it on occasion with such force that it causes sudden storms to erupt upon the earth.

Zamiel

From the Book of Enoch. Zamiel is the angel of hurricanes. This angel was fascinated with God's creation of the water upon the earth and often enjoys playing with the substance, sometimes with a little too much enthusiasm, which results in what we know as hurricanes.

Zephon

Found in a number of books of questionable authorship, this angel is often associated with fire. Supposedly, the angel Zephon was one of the many angels of heaven who was lured into Lucifer's plot to overthrow God in what has become to be known as The War in Heaven. Zephon's primary mission in the battle was setting heaven on fire. However, before he could conceive a plan and method of accomplishing this task, Lucifer's forces lost their celestial battle and he, and all who had joined him in his rebellion were cast out of heaven and into the pits of hell. As punishment for his part in the plot, Zephon is forced to beat his wings constantly to fan the fires of hell.

ANGELIC
ENCOUNTERS
ACROSS AMERICA

ALABAMA

The Angel and the Chevy

IT WAS A typical summer day in the town of Tuscaloosa, Alabama. The sweltering heat of August, mixed with a high humidity that enveloped a person like a wet blanket, made even the simplest task a sweat-drenched ordeal. But for Robert Irving, a black mill worker and father of seven children, the repairing of his broken-down 1969 Chevy pickup was a necessity. He worked the late shift at the mill and could not afford to miss a single day's pay, not with a wife and seven kids to feed.

The Irving family did not have a lot, materially that is: the old pickup had over three hundred thousand miles on it and had belonged to Robert's father. After his death it had passed on to the eldest son. Their house had only two bedrooms, with a back porch converted into a third, which was shared by Robert's four sons, the eldest of whom was fourteen-year-old Robert, Jr. Three daughters shared the second bedroom. It was a little cramped at times, but the Irvings had made do with what they had. What Robert and his wife Josephine lacked in material things, they made up for with plenty of love and a strong Christian belief which they had passed on to their children.

Struggling to place a bolt into the transmission from underneath the old pickup, Robert Irving heard his son's voice. "Daddy, Mama says for you to take a break and drink some of this lemonade before you pass out from the heat."

Sliding out from under the truck, Robert, Sr. wiped the sweat from his face and smiled with pride at his oldest boy. "Well, thank you, son. Your ma's right as always—mighty hot under this old truck."

"Daddy, don't you get tired of fixin' this old thing all the time. You oughta get another one," said Robert, Jr.

Robert smiled. "Cost money, son. This here truck's been a good one for a lot of years. It just needs some help sometimes that's all. Just like people."

"Yeah, it's been needin' a lot lately," said Robert, Jr., with a grin. "Don't you ever get mad—I mean real mad and want to cuss it or kick it, or somethin'?"

Robert shook his head "Oh, I suppose I feel that way sometimes, but then what good would that do? The truck would still be broke and I'd still have to fix her, right?"

"Yeah, I suppose you're right. But, Pa, do you ever feel like God sometimes has put a lot on us?

I mean, like this old truck, and you and Mama havin' to work so hard all the time." Robert, Jr. lowered his head and his voice trailed off a bit as he said, "I don't know—sometimes it just don't seem fair."

Robert reached out and took his son's hand. "Son, it isn't about being fair or not, it's what you feel in your heart. God done gave me seven healthy, strong children, I think that's more than bein' fair. And this old truck, well that's just God's way of testin' my patience from time to time."

Young Robert mentioned that the Lord sure had been doing a lot of patience testing of late, then went back into the house as his father slid back under the old truck to continue his work.

Twenty minutes later, young Robert came back onto the porch. His dad was still under the truck. Young Robert was suddenly overcome with a terrible premonition. It was as if someone or something was drawing him off the porch and to the front of the truck. He could not explain it and was understandably a little frightened of this strange and inexplicable feeling, but he did not resist it.

His father was still working and didn't realize the boy was there. Young Robert's eyes were drawn to the front bumper of the truck and the old jack that held the vehicle a good two feet off the ground. The following sequence of events occurred within a matter of seconds, but to young Robert they seemed to happen in slow motion. From somewhere behind him the boy felt a gentle touch on his shoulder which turned him around and moved him toward a large piece of firewood on a stack by the side of the house. "Pick it up, Robert," said a soft and gentle voice from out of nowhere. The boy did as instructed. "Place it under the bumper, Robert, hurry!" said the voice with a sense of urgency.

Moving quickly, the boy stood the piece of cordwood upright under the bumper next to the jack. No sooner had he removed his hands from the wood, when the jack slipped and fell sideways. Robert, Sr. yelled. Realizing what had happened, he expected to be crushed by the weight of the vehicle coming down on top of him. But it didn't. The sturdy piece of wood had been placed perfectly and the old truck had fallen only a matter of inches.

Scrambling out from under his truck, Robert Irving saw his son's frightened face. Moving quickly to the front of the truck, the father stared down at the piece of wood that had saved his life. Grabbing his son, he pulled him close and said, "My God, son! You've saved my life. How'd you know that jack was going to fall?"

Still a little shaken, young Robert told his father about feeling the hand on his shoulder and the voice that had spoke to him only moments before the jack fell. The father held his son even tighter, convinced that God's guardian angel had directed his son's actions that afternoon.

The Stranger on the Shore

DONNA MARKS, FROM Decatur, Alabama, was seventeen years old and a senior in high school, looking forward to her upcoming graduation only three weeks away. After a relaxed summer of new found freedom, she would go on to the University of Alabama and a whole new world of education. To say she was excited by the coming events in her young life would have been an understatement.

For the weekend, Donna and a large portion of her senior class were going to Wheeler Lake for a day of fun. There would be swimming, waterskiing, hamburgers, and hot dogs. It was going to be a great day. Soon a car full of kids pulled up in front of the house and honked its horn. Donna kissed her mother on the cheek and she raced out the door. Her mother reminded her to be careful and to try and be home by dark. "Okay, Mom. Don't worry," said Donna.

Everyone seemed to be at the lake that day. Even some of the stuffy old teachers had showed up in their Bermuda shorts and colorful shirts as if to demonstrate to the kids that even they were human when it came to a day at the lake. By noon the whole party was in full swing. Donna's boyfriend, John, had sweet talked his father into letting him take the family boat, complete with skis and a water board. Soon, all the kids were lining up for a chance to show their skiing abilities in front of their peers. Donna and two of her girl friends were in the boat with John. It was a great day for skiing. The sun was bright and warm, and the breeze blowing in their faces as the boat flew across the water was exhilarating. It was one of those days that made a person feel wonderfully alive.

By that afternoon, everyone had had a turn on the skis, everyone that is, except Donna. At first she refused, she wasn't really that good at skiing. Although John had been teaching her all last summer, she was still pretty shaky on the boards. But soon, with the encouragement of John and her two girl friends, Donna rather reluctantly slipped over the side of the boat and took hold of the ski line. "Now, not too fast, Johnny," she said as the boat began to ease forward. She allowed the tow line to slide through her hand until she came to the handle attached at the end. Positioning herself in the water and with the handle grasped securely in both hands, she yelled, "Okay Johnny." Under her breath she whispered, "Oh God, why am I doing this?"

John gunned the powerful boat forward, its momentum pulling Donna up and out of the water. Trying to remember to keep her knees bent and a hundred other tips John had tried to teach her, she managed to stay on her feet. The water spraying up into her face mixed with the wind felt good to her. She was doing it, she was skiing. Those in the boat were cheering her success. John couldn't resist towing her along a strip of the lake in front of the class so they could all witness his successful training program. Everyone cheered Donna as she went flying by. She started to wave, then almost fell, and quickly grabbing the handle she realized she wasn't all that good just yet.

Swinging the boat back out to the center of the lake, John began to accelerate. Donna could feel the increased power of the boat and the wind in her face. Her control began to waver and her knees shake. This was too fast and she knew it. John suddenly made a sharp turn, increasing the girl's speed even more as she swung wide. She tried to yell to John slow down, but her words were useless over the roar of the boat's powerful motor and the howling wind in her face.

Another turn swung Donna in a wide loop, sending her toward a shoreline strewn with rocks and fallen trees. As the trees went flying by, she saw a young man suddenly appear from out of the treeline. He stood silently watching her as she went past. A sudden wave almost sent her legs out from under her. "Oh God," whispered Donna. She started to let go of the rope but she wasn't certain how deep the water was. She'd wait until John swung back out away from the shoreline then let go.

Donna's decision of when to let go of the rope was suddenly and unexpectedly taken away from her. A large tree limb, adrift in the water, bobbed up directly in front of her. A more skilled skier could have avoided the obstruction, but Donna was not yet that proficient. Leaning back on her skis, she braced herself for the coming impact. The tips of the skis were pointed up enough to give them lift over the limb, but Donna went sailing into the air as if launched from a missile pad. High into the air she went, her skis flying in different directions. She believes she screamed, but can't really remember. The speed of the boat at the time of impact catapulted the girl over thirty feet into the air. When she came down, she came down hard. She landed flat on her back. The impact of the water knocked the breath out of her and pain shot through every muscle of her body.

Donna can remember sinking into the depths of the water. There was nothing she could do. Her arms felt as if they were paralyzed. Panic set in. She felt as though she were suffocating. She couldn't get any air. There was only the feeling of the water closing in around her and a darkness closing in over her pain-filled eyes. To Donna Marks there was no doubt that she was about to die.

It was then that she felt a strong hand clasp her around the waist and begin carrying her upward toward the surface. At the same instant a strange calm came over her. Gone was the sense of fear and panic. Half dazed, she felt a breeze on her face as she broke the surface and inhaled deeply of the sweet smelling air. Her breathing began to return to normal and she turned about in the water to find her rescuer, but there was no one there. She was totally alone in the water.

Thirty yards to her left, John was heading the boat back for her. The girls in the boat were holding their hands to their faces in complete terror. They just knew Donna had drowned. When John pulled the boat alongside Donna and helped her into the craft he was apologizing from the moment he arrived. But Donna didn't hear a word he was saying. If the boat had not reached her until now, who had brought her back up to the surface? Who had saved her life? Her eyes went to the shoreline in search of the young man she had seen there only seconds before the accident. There was no one there. "Where did that man go that was standing on the shore?" she asked.

Her friends looked questioningly at each other. Neither John nor the two girls had seen anyone on the shore. They were the only people on or near that part of the lake.

ALASKA

The Tower Angel

TERRY BALDWIN HAD been flying hunters, tourists, and adventurers to all parts of Alaska for fifteen years. Operating his charter service out of Fairbanks, he had managed to make a comfortable living for his family. For Terry, Alaska was the last true wilderness left in America and he and his family loved the country. The thought of living anywhere else had never been mentioned since their arrival in the snowbound state fifteen years earlier.

Terry was an experienced pilot, having earned his wings as a navy pilot during the Vietnam War. He had flown everything from choppers to top speed jet fighters. After parting company with the Navy, he went on to a variety of flying jobs, from shuttling cargo across the country to being a chopper jockey for a radio station. It was not until he watched a television special about Alaska that he knew what he really wanted to do and where. Pooling all their money and selling their house, the Baldwins headed to Alaska where flying is practically the only way to get anywhere outside the boundaries of the big cities.

One day in late March 1992, the Reverend Paul Roberts came to Terry and requested to charter his plane for a trip to Anchorage where the new pastor of the church was due to arrive. Reverend Roberts wanted to be on hand to personally greet his new replacement. Terry assured him that there was no problem and since he had two hunters that he had planned to fly there anyway, the pastor's flight would be on the house. They would leave the following morning.

Terry was at the airfield early and had everything ready to go when his passengers arrived. Weather conditions were not the best. A snow storm was closing in on Fairbanks, but they should be clear of it before it started moving in. When everyone was buckled in, Terry headed the twin-engine Cessna down the runway and lifted gracefully up into the Alaskan sky and headed toward Anchorage.

An hour into the flight Terry noticed a storm cell moving in from the west. If this was the storm the tower had told him about, it was definitely way off the projected path. Although not really concerned about this new turn of events, Terry contacted the Fairbanks tower and reported his sighting. The tower informed him that this was a new front that had come out of nowhere and that Anchorage was already feeling the brunt of the storm. They suggested that Terry turn back for Fairbanks and wait until the weather cleared. Terry relayed this information to his passengers and asked how they felt about the situation. Did they want to turn back?

The two hunters had no objection, it would give them a little more time to party in Alaska. Reverend Roberts also agreed. This flight had been more of a good will mission than a necessity anyway. "Okay," said Terry, "we're heading back for Fairbanks."

Terry contacted the tower and notified them of his change of plans. They informed him that he had better hurry; the original storm was moving in faster than they had anticipated and it looked as if it was going to be a bad one. Terry rogered the message. They'd be back over Fairbanks in less than one hour. At this point no one was that concerned, although the two hunters did seem to be talking less and Reverend Roberts had removed his Bible from his small carry-on bag and was now reading silently to himself.

Thirty minutes out of Fairbanks, Terry noticed his instrument panel began showing a series of strange readings and his compass was rocking wildly, unable to stabilize on a stationary direction. His altitude showed they were flying four thousand feet higher than the setting he had been at only moments ago. That was impossible. He hadn't touched the yoke. Looking out his left window, Terry could see the mountainous white clouds of the storm closing in on them. Already, wet flakes of snow were striking the cockpit window. In a matter of minutes they were going to be in the center of this storm and with instruments that were, if not totally unreliable, at least questionable. Terry began a rapid recheck of his equipment. He could find nothing wrong, yet there had to be something.

Trying to maintain his control, Terry calmly radioed the tower. "Fairbanks, this is Cessna 4Y Whiskey Delta Seven. I'm having a little problem with my instruments. Do you have us on your radar at this time? Over." "4Y Whiskey Delta Seven, this is Fairbanks Tower—Roger, I have you five-zero miles southsoutheast at ten thousand feet, over."

Terry, still remaining calm, told the tower that his instruments showed him at fifteen thousand feet and southwest of Fairbanks.

"Sounds like you have a problem, 4Y Whiskey Delta Seven. I suggest you abandon all reliability on your instruments and we'll talk you down. Do you roger this?"

"Affirmative, Fairbanks."

The air control guided Terry's small craft to a lower altitude then gave him a new heading to line him up with the runway still forty miles away. One of the hunters asked if they in effect were now flying blind. Terry assured him there was nothing to worry about. Fairbanks' radar was as good as a pair of eyes.

Within a few minutes the on-rushing storm began to obscure Terry's vision. The snow coming in wet sheets was covering the windshield with a blanket of flakes. They really were flying blind now. There was total silence within the confines of the small aircraft as they winged their way toward Fairbanks.

"4Y Whiskey Delta Seven, this is tower. You are drifting to your left. Bring it back slowly until I tell you to stop."

Terry did as instructed. In all his years of flying in Alaska he had never seen a storm as thick as this one. Turbulence began rocking and bumping the Cessna, adding a sudden rush of adrenaline to his blood every time it happened. Terry was beginning to think it couldn't get much worse, but he was wrong. He knew the rocking turbulence had pushed him off to the left again but the tower hadn't responded to the change in course. Keying his microphone, he requested a correction on his flight path. There was a long silence. He made another request. Again there was nothing from the tower. Where were they? Why didn't they answer?

Terry was beginning to get rattled now. Desperately he made three more calls, but still the Fairbanks tower did not answer. The veteran pilot could hear Reverend Roberts whispering the Lord's Prayer. The two hunters quickly joined in.

Terry pounded on the instrument panel as if by some form of magic the assault would somehow correct whatever was wrong with the gauges. It had no effect, they were still spinning wildly and totally useless to the small plane flying blindly through the storm. Terry looked at his watch. The tower had said he was fifty miles out from Fairbanks. That had been fifteen minutes ago. By his best estimates Terry figured they were now less than twenty-five miles from their destination—that was if they were still going in the right direction. The winds suddenly shifted and Terry found the Cessna now fighting a strong headwind. This new development would have a radical effect on their fuel. Ironically, the only instrument that appeared to be working correctly was the fuel gauge, and it showed a steady drop. There was no turning back now, there wasn't enough fuel to go anywhere but Fairbanks.

It was a desperate situation. Terry wasn't sure how high they were flying, which direction they were heading, or how far away they were from the airfield. Reverend Roberts leaned forward and asked that Terry try the radio again. Why not? What did they have to lose?

"Fairbanks Tower, this is 4Y Delta. Do you read me? Over."

There was a strained moment of silence, then sudden relief as Terry and the others heard the composed voice of the controller's voice breaking the silence of the cockpit. "If you will listen to me, I can get you into Fairbanks and down."

"Roger, tower, go ahead," answered Terry with renewed enthusiasm.

The controller began giving instructions. "Bring it down just a little. Now pull to the right until I tell you to stop." Terry followed each order intently.

"Stop there," said the controller. "Now, down . . . down . . . down. Hold it right there."

Reverend Roberts and the two hunters were praying openly now. Thanking God that the tower had been able to pick them up despite the storm, the three men sat on the edges of their seats staring occasionally at the gas gauge as it plummeted toward empty before their very eyes. Only the calm authority of the voice coming over the radio stayed off sheer panic among them.

"Bring her up a bit now. No, you're too far to the left. That's better." Terry's face was drenched in sweat. This was turning out to be the longest flight of his life. Would it ever end?

Suddenly, the controller said, "You're coming in on the end of the runway. Ease it down ... down. Okay, set it down ... now!"

With nothing but faith in a voice on a radio, Terry obediently dropped the Cessna down through the surrounding whiteness. Then, suddenly, as if by magic, Terry saw the beginning of the runway just ahead, with lights lining both sides. Within a few seconds they touched down and a wild cheer broke among the passengers.

The plane taxied to a stop, and the four men offered a quick prayer of thanks to the Almighty. Terry's body felt as if it were tied in knots. Slumping back against the seat, he keyed his mike and in a shaky voice said, "Thanks tower. There's little doubt that you saved our lives today."

The controller's reply cast a stunned silence over the men in the plane. "What are you talking about? We lost contact with you about forty miles out."

"You what?" asked Terry.

"Roger, Cessna. We lost radio contact with you at forty miles and radar contact when you were less than twenty miles out. We thought you'd went down in the storm. We never heard you talking to us or anyone else," said the controller. "We were surprised to see you reappear on the radar just before you dropped down out of those clouds. You boys must have had the angels on your side today. But whatever happened, we're glad you're down and safe. Have a nice day, 4Y Whiskey Delta."

A stunned Terry turned to his passengers. Speechless, they could only shake their heads. Even Reverend Roberts seemed overwhelmed by the controller's words. Had the controller been right? Were the angels with 4Y Whiskey Delta that day? It seems clear . . . someone or something had been with them.

ARIZONA

An Angel's Guidance

THE SUNSET WAS shrouded by black clouds. Lightning cracked and torrents of rain fell. It was the worst storm to hit Mesa, Arizona, in almost a decade. From her second-story window Diane Mowry could see stalled cars caught in the flash flooding that was sending cascades of water moving rapidly down the streets of Mesa. A lone station wagon struggled through the racing waters and headed up Diane's street. It stopped for a moment in front of her house, then struggled to make the turn into the Mowry's driveway. The swift water almost carried the car sideways as it made the turn, but fortunately the front wheel drive vehicle's front tires caught on the incline of the driveway and pulled the car up into the safety of the driveway. Diane raced downstairs to open the front door.

Two teenage girls dashed from the car to the front door. Shivering and soaking wet, one of the girls asked, "May I use your phone? I need to call my father and tell him we're okay."

"Of course," said Diane. "Please come in."

Diane showed the girls where they could make their call, then went into the kitchen to fix some hot cocoa. In the kitchen she found her husband Paul pacing the floor. The newspaper office where he worked was flooding and he was waiting for a call from the facility manager. "Norm is at home," said Paul, "and he promised to check in with me about conditions at the office. Why hasn't he called yet?"

The girls finished their call, and Paul stopped pacing.

"My dad said to wait out the storm here," one teen said as she sipped her warm cocoa. "He was a little worried about our being in a stranger's house, so I gave him your number. Was that all right?"

"Of course, dear," replied Diane. "Tell me, what made you stop in front of our house as you were coming down the street?"

The driver of the car answered. "It was a couple of things. One, I could feel the car beginning to hydroplane from the force of the water and knew we had to get out of the main flow. And second"—the girl paused for a moment staring at her cup of cocoa, then at Diane—"you may think this sounds crazy, but when I saw your house I heard a voice telling me to stop and turn in here. I have no idea why, but I just did it."

Diane and Paul exchanged curious glances at the young girl's remark. Just then the phone rang. Paul went to answer it. After a few seconds he returned.

"That was Norm," he said, "but he wasn't calling to tell me about the condition of the office." A strange look came over his face as he continued. "He wanted to thank me for keeping his daughter and her friend safe during the storm."

Norm's daughter had never met Paul or Diane Mowry, let alone knew where those people lived. Yet, when they were facing impending danger from the rising water, a voice from nowhere directed them to the safe haven of the Mowrys'.

The Desert Angel

THE YELLOW PIPER Cub roared down the small
runway of Needles, California, and headed east.
Phil Hayden had filed his flight plan for a trip to
Prescott, Arizona. It was a perfect day for flying
and Hayden, who had only had his pilot's li-
cense for a few months was looking forward to
the solo flight and the peaceful tranquility he
found while flying like an eagle through the sky.

Soon he passed over the Sacramento Wash and
the small community of Yucca, Arizona. Loom-
ing below were the vast desert wastelands of the
Mohave; miles upon miles of scorching heat and
sand that seem to stretch to the horizon. An earlier weather report had stated that on this day
the Mohave would reach an unbelievable 130 degrees.

One hour out of Needles, everything seemed
to be going fine. Phil Hayden was listening to his
favorite music station broadcasting out of Phoe-
nix and the Piper was purring like a kitten. Vis-
ibility was unlimited and there wasn't a cloud in
the sky. At first Phil hadn't taken much notice of

the small dust devil that was swirling across the
desert floor only a few miles ahead of him. Then
why should he? It was down there and he was
eight thousand feet up in the sky.

Phil turned away from the cockpit for only a
moment to reach for a container of bottled water
he had in a small ice chest behind the passenger
seat. When he turned back around he was startled to find a huge whirling circle of wind and
sand directly in his flight path. Before he could
react, the small Piper penetrated the outer circle
of the small cyclone and was tossed about like a
toy. Phil's heart raced as he was almost thrown
out of his seat. The Piper bounced and shook as
if it would come apart any second. The powerful
whirling sand grated against the metal of the ex-
terior, stripping away huge patches of yellow
paint. "Oh, God!" whispered Phil, "help me,
please."

Suddenly, the plane broke from the storm and
into the clear blue skies once more. Clearly
shaken by his ordeal, Phil dropped back in his
seat and wiped the sweat from his frightened
face. He had often heard about those types of
whirlwinds but this was the first one he had ever
encountered.

Phil's relief was short lived. The Piper suddenly began to sputter as the engine coughed
twice, then labored to come back to life. "Oh Jesus, what now?" Again the engine sputtered
twice, cleared itself, then sputtered again, only
this time the engine stopped. In panic and shock
Phil stared out from the cockpit at the mo-

tionless propeller that hung like a brightly colored stick from the front of his plane. Phil Hayden was going down.

In desperation he fought to remember what his instructor had told him about a dead stick landing and how to glide a Piper from a forced landing. Surprisingly, his hands automatically began performing the procedures as if this was an everyday occurrence. Regaining his confidence, Phil searched the ground below for any sign of a town or house, even a highway, anything that showed signs of life. But he could see nothing but desert below him. The weather prediction of 130 degrees suddenly came to mind. How long could he possibly last in that kind of heat in the middle of nowhere? If the landing didn't kill him, it was a good bet that the desert would. Phil Hayden began to pray as the small Piper made its way toward the desert floor below.

"Oh mighty God, I know I don't give thanks to you as often as I should, and for that I ask your forgiveness. I am really in need of your help here, God. If you can see your way clear to somehow help me—not a day shall ever pass again that I do not give you the recognition you deserve."

The Piper had dropped to an altitude of five thousand feet when Phil's heart skipped a beat. Just beyond a small hill he spied a single building and an old makeshift runway. There were two gas pumps standing alongside the building. Overjoyed at the sight, he nosed the Piper around and glided her down onto the cracked and rutted hardtop of the old runway. His breathing did not return to normal until the plane had come to a dead stop. Leaning his head on the wheel, he gave a word of thanks.

Opening the door, Phil felt a rush of sweltering heat hit him square in the face. It was a drastic change from the air conditioned cockpit. Stepping out of the plane, he looked around for any signs of life, but saw no one. Undoing the hood that covered the engine, he began to inspect it for damage, but Phil wasn't a mechanic. He wouldn't have known what was wrong with the aircraft if he saw it.

"Piper Cub. Nice little planes, yes sirree," said a voice from out of nowhere.

Startled, Phil twirled to see an old man in his late sixties or seventies, with salt-and-pepper hair and a leathery face, smiling at him through a chew of tobacco that looked like a small golf ball in the side of his cheek. Judging from the dirty, grease stained coveralls and T-shirt the old fellow wore, he did some type of mechanical work. "Got a problem do you, boy?" asked the old man.

"I surely do," said Phil, and went on to tell of his experience with the sudden sand storm and the effect it had on his plane. "Do you think you might be able to fix it?" asked Phil hopefully.

"Well let's take a look at her. Sounds like you got sand in the fuel system. Why don't you go on up to the shop there and get you a soda? It's air-conditioned in there. I'll see what I can do about your plane. No sense in you standin' around out here in this heat."

The old man seemed to have a calm, relaxing effect on Phil. Feeling the heat, he took the man's advice and went to the shop building. Entering the cool air of the room, he found some soda stuck in washtub of ice. He downed half of the drink before he realized it. His mouth had been like cotton ever since the engine had started sputtering.

In about an hour the old man came up to the shop. "Just like I figured, sand in the fuel system. I cleared the lines and cleaned the carburetor. That oughta take care of it. You might want to get her checked a little better whenever you get where you're goin'."

Phil could hardly find the words to express his thanks to the old man. "How much do I owe you?" he asked.

"Oh nothin' at all son. Wasn't much to it really and I wasn't doin' anything important anyway. Glad to help you out. You be careful now. I'll be seein' ya."

Phil stood stunned. This man had practically saved his life and didn't want anything for it. That wouldn't be right, said Phil, insisting that the old man take some token of payment, but again he refused. "Why don't you take another one of them sodas along with you," said the mechanic, "got plenty more of 'em in the back."

Phil smiled, "Okay, but I insist on paying you something before I leave." Reaching into the tub, Phil pulled out another soda, when he turned back around the old man was gone. Searching the area, Phil could not find him anywhere. Mystified by the old man's strange behavior, Phil climbed into the Piper and hit the ignition switch. The small plane roared to life immediately and hummed just as well as the day it came out of the factory. Taking one last look from out of the cockpit for the old man, but seeing nothing, Phil eased the plane around and within minutes was once again cruising the clear blue skies over Arizona. Within two hours he was receiving landing instructions from the Prescott control tower. Once on the ground he reported directly to the operations center. They wanted to talk to him about the unexpected change in his flight plan.

The director and one of the controllers of the flight center listened intently to Phil's story. The director shook his head as he sat back in his swivel chair. "That's quite a story, Mr. Hayden. We had a report of that storm from some other pilots. We figured you might have went down out there somewhere and needed help. You hadn't showed up when you did we were about to send out a search plane to look for you. But, we're glad you're here and safe."

Phil could see a look of doubt in the man's face. "Well, like I said, if it hadn't been for that old man that lives out at that old runway, I would have been in a lot of trouble, that's for sure. Is there any way I can get some money sent out to him before I leave? He wouldn't take it while I was there."

The two men of the flight center stared at each other for a minute, then the controller asked, "How long did say you were on the ground, Mr. Hayden?"

"About an hour. Why?"

"Well, sir. An hour on the ground in 130 degree heat can affect people in a lot of different ways. The heat makes you see things that aren't really there, you know what I mean?"

Phil came out of his chair. "What do you mean—see things? Are you trying to tell me I'm lying about going down, or what?"

The director moved quickly to calm Phil down and asked him to be seated again. "Mr. Hayden, no one is saying that you are lying about anything, it's just that . . . well, sir, that runway you're talking about hasn't been used since the end of World War Two and there hasn't been anyone living at that old place for over forty years."

Phil Hayden hasn't missed a Sunday in church since that day. And whenever the subject of angels comes up, and others imagine them with white robes and wings, Phil envisions one with a leathery face, dirty old overalls, and a smile that he will remember for the rest of his life.

ARKANSAS

Angel of the Fire

LATE ONE MARCH evening in 1974, Jerry Bond was awakened by the sound of distant cries and shouts. At first he thought it was a domestic dispute, but an urgency in the voices caused him to think that it might be more than that. He got out of bed and opened his bedroom window. The smell of smoke, heavy and pungent, drifted into the room. Down the street, the voices, shrill with panic, cut clearly through the cool night air.

"Help me! Help me! My little girl! My little girl is in there!"

Realizing someone was in trouble, Jerry pulled his pants on, grabbed a flashlight, and raced out of the house and down the street where the screams were coming from. Once there, he saw a one-story brick house belonging to a family named Green in flames. Black smoke was pouring out of the windows. A small crowd had gathered, mostly neighbors and a few policemen. The fire department hadn't arrived yet.

In the flickering orange-black darkness, Jerry watched in horror as a team of men struggled to pull Mr. Green, severely burned and in a state of shock, through a small window near the back of the house. Then he saw Mrs. Green and three of her children huddled together on the front lawn. Their faces mirrored the fear and terror that was erupting all around them. Mrs. Green was nearly hysterical.

"Theresa!" she screamed. "My Theresa is still in there!"

I've got to do something, thought Jerry. *I've got to help*. But he stood there frozen, unable to move. Confusion and panic surrounded him, became a part of him. The entire atmosphere seemed to crackle with the heat and tension. He was afraid. A shower of fiery sparks lit up the night time sky as a part of the house caved in, and he heard Mrs. Green scream again.

"O Lord," Jerry prayed. "Please help me." And with that, Jerry rushed toward the house and pushed his way through the first available window. Once inside, he could hardly see. His heart was pounding like a drum. Everything was engulfed in black and smoke.

He groped his way forward until he was half-way across the room. Then abruptly, he stopped. Something—some strong and strange sensation—told him that he was in the wrong room. "This isn't right," it seemed to say. "This isn't where you'll find her." The feeling was so powerful that Jerry couldn't shake it. And then, on his shoulder, he felt the firm grasp of a hand pulling him back toward the window.

"Get out of here!" he yelled, fearing for the other person's life. He turned to see who it was but there was no one there. No one but Jerry, alone and trembling.

Gasping, he headed for the window, pulled himself out, and lowered himself to the ground. He looked up to see Mrs. Green's frantic eyes desperately searching his for encouragement. Finding none there, she gestured wildly toward another window.

"There," she screamed hoarsely. "Go in there."

The window was a few feet off the ground. Someone gave Jerry a lift up and he pushed himself inside, dropping to the floor with a thud. This room, too, was dark and smoldering. His eyes were burning. He could barely see an arm's length in front of himself.

"O Lord," he prayed again, "please help me. Guide me."

What happened next left Jerry Bond momentarily stunned. First, as if in answer to his prayer, he felt a surge of confidence that he was in the right place, that he would find Theresa. Then, to his amazement he felt the return of the same firm force on his shoulder that he had felt in the other room. This time, however, it was even stronger and it seemed to push him to the floor. Although Jerry didn't understand what was happening, he never fought it. Instinctively, he allowed this force to take over. Its presence was both calming and reassuring. Something within him knew that whatever it was, it was good.

He relaxed and let himself be guided to the floor. He began to crawl, following the wall, arms outstretched, reaching, grabbing. He came to a bed and raised himself to search its rumpled surface. "No!" a voice seemed to warn. "Stay low!" He returned to the crawling position on the floor. He had found nothing in the bed. "Don't worry," whispered the strange voice, "you're almost there. Don't worry."

At the foot of the bed lay a pile of charred chairs, quilts, and blankets that seemed to have been thrown to the floor by someone in a panic. Reaching deep into the tangled maze, Jerry felt what he had been looking for—an arm, a leg, it was impossible to tell—but he knew he had found Theresa. He pulled and pulled until she emerged from the pile, a limp little brown-haired bundle. She was badly burned.

"Theresa?" he whispered.

A shuddering gasp confirmed that she was still alive. Jerry eased her small body over his shoulder and moved for the window.

The crowd outside stared in silence as he gently laid the little girl on the ground and began to administer mouth-to-mouth resuscitation. Her small face, black with soot and burns, held no expression. Blue lights from the police cars cast a strange, pulsating glow over the scene. As Jerry continued to try and breathe life into the girl's tiny frame he prayed that she would live. Wailing sirens and flashing red lights signaled the arrival of the fire department. Jerry continued his task as he heard the fire chief on his bullhorn shouting orders. He heard the front door being kicked down. The fire, fueled by the rush of fresh oxygen, exploded with a scorching blast. At that same instant, Theresa's eyelids fluttered. She was breathing on her own. Jerry held her until the ambulance arrived.

"Looks like you got to her just in time," said the medic, as he took her from Jerry's arms. "She's burned pretty bad, but she'll make it, thanks to you."

Jerry walked with the medic to the ambulance. He watched as they carefully placed the little girl inside and drove away. Not till the ambulance was out of sight did Jerry Bond go home.

Shaken by the experience, plagued by the smell of burning flesh and the echoes of screams, Jerry couldn't sleep. More than anything else, he was completely and totally unnerved by the mysterious presence that had led him to the little girl. Jerry had always had faith in God and the power of prayer, but this kind of intervention seemed uncanny—too close for comfort—at least for a guy like him. The idea was almost too much to comprehend, but he couldn't dismiss it either. It had happened. It kept him up the rest of the night.

At 7:00 A.M. Jerry put on his shoes and jacket and returned to the scene of the fire. The house was nothing more than a charred hull of blackened brick. Smoke still rose from the remains. Skeletal shells of smoking furniture were strewn around the front yard. The fire inspector was there with a few policemen. They asked why Jerry was there. He told them. The fire inspector said that the fire may have been caused by a cigarette left burning near the living room sofa.

Jerry went around to the room where he had found Theresa. Like the rest of the house, it was badly charred and blackened from the smoke. The walls were blistered from the intense heat. In one corner rested the remains of a melted tennis racket.

Slowly Jerry turned to gaze around the gutted room. Suddenly he stopped, transfixed, his eyes riveted on the wall. There directly above the spot where he had found Theresa, was a print, neatly hung and strangely, the only thing in the room undamaged by the fire. The frame, to be sure, was black with soot, but the picture was clear and untouched. Jerry recognized the subject by the walking stick and the water gourd slung over the figure's shoulder. It was the wandering traveler who is particularly fond of the young—the guardian angel Raphael.

CALIFORNIA

A Promise Kept

IT WAS A sad time in the town of Clovis, California, for the Martin family. Thora Martin had passed away during the night after a long illness, leaving behind a loving husband and daughter. Liza Martin and her mother had always been close. Although the doctors had informed the family months before that Thora's condition was terminal, her actual death had been hard for Liza to accept. Cleaning and straightening the room where her mother had spent her last days, Liza discovered a small journal beside the bedstand. Opening it she read the last entry. In it her mother had written: "When God calls me home, I will let you know when I have arrived on the other side. The message will come either on the day I leave or on the day of the funeral, I'll ask God to send a storm as a sign that I am with him."

Liza showed the entry to her father and both

agreed to keep it within the family for the time being. Liza reminded her father that it had drizzled on the day her mother had died. Could that have been the sign? Surely not. A drizzle was hardly a storm.

On the day of Thora's funeral, Liza and her father were disappointed to see clear blue skies and bright sunshine. The funeral home was filled with people who remembered Thora Martin fondly. After the service at the church, the motorcade made its way through the small town on its way to the gravesite. The summer had never been brighter or warmer than it was that day.

At the gravesite, Mr. Martin asked that one of the ministers read aloud Thora Martin's last entry in her journal. Now everyone knew about it.

That afternoon, a luncheon was held on the back patio of the Martin home. By 5:00 P.M. most of the guests had departed and Liza busied herself cleaning up. Pausing, she stared up at the clear sky, the disappointment apparent in her face. At that moment a well-dressed young man that Liza had never seen before came up to her. His voice was soft and peaceful as he quietly said, "Do not give up hope, Liza."

Liza started to reply, but before she could say anything the young man walked away. Turning to her father she asked, "Dad, who is that young man walking away?"

Liza's father turned and looked in the direction his daughter was pointing, but there was no one there. "What man?" asked her father. Liza looked around the patio and the yard, but the man was nowhere to be found. "Never mind, Dad. I guess I'm just getting a little tired."

Carrying a load of glasses and plates into the kitchen, Liza couldn't shake the thought of the young man from her mind. How strange. He had only said six words and then was gone. Opening the dishwasher, Liza began putting the glasses inside. Suddenly she heard a rumble that sounded like an army marching through heaven. Black clouds suddenly rolled across the skies. Lightning darted through the clouds. Liza rushed outside and looked toward the heavens as rain began to fall in wind-blown sheets. Rain, mixed with her tears, poured down the woman's face.

That afternoon the lights went out in the house. Lightning struck the front of Mr. Martin's store, setting off the burglar alarm which rang loud and clear for a few minutes. Then the power at the store also went out. Weathermen could not explain the sudden arrival of this storm.

That evening the Martins' phone rang off the hook. They were calls from people that had found hope in the storm. Between answering the wave of calls, Liza thought of the young man she had met that afternoon. Who was he really? Then she laughed. Liza couldn't help thinking of how appropriate it was for her mother, whose name, Thora, means "the thunderer."

The Roll of Comfort

THE FIRST DAY her husband, Lynn, received che-
motherapy, Nancy Bayless of San Diego, California, was overwhelmed with sadness. They lived
on a boat, and that night Nancy worried about
her husband and all the responsibilities that fell
upon her shoulders.

At midnight, as she was preparing for bed,
Nancy ran out of paper towels. In the darkness
of the main cabin she found a double package
stowed away in a locker. She ripped open the
cellophane and took out a roll. She always
bought plain white to go with their red-white-
and-blue decor. When she turned on the light she
could see that this roll was covered with pink
flowers—that was all wrong. It was supposed to
be white!

This simple discovery triggered the release of
a host of worries and frustration that she had
fought to hold in herself far too long. Staring at
the flowered paper, Nancy slumped down at the
table and burst into tears. "Lord, I can't even buy
the right paper towels. How will I ever manage

everything else?" she cried. "How will I varnish the boat? Take care of the engine? How will I ever go on without Lynn?"

Nancy remained at the table until her tears were spent. Satisfied that she had wallowed long enough in her self-pity, she picked up the roll of paper towels, and as she was putting them into the holder she noticed that there was writing among the flowers. One sheet read "Friendship is a special gift." The words made her think of all the friends she could call on at any hour of the day or night. The next sheet read "Love is sharing." Tears filled Nancy's eyes again as she thought of the gifts they had been given—casseroles, cookies, gentle words, and a hundred hugs. Then came "No act of love however small is ever wasted." This message reminded her of the phone calls and other acts of kindness she had received. Setting the roll aside, Nancy suddenly felt as if there was another presence in the galley with her. It gave her a calm and peaceful feeling.

Nancy went to bed that night and slept her most restful sleep since the whole ordeal of Lynn's illness had begun. The following morning Nancy opened the locker again. Inside the torn cellophane was the second roll of paper towels, but when she removed this roll, she found that there were no flowers, no printing. The roll was a plain white.

COLORADO

The Stranger on
the Mountain

EARL WEAVER AND Ted Monroe lived in the Denver area all their lives. Their favorite sport was mountain climbing and the two teenagers never missed an opportunity to head for the mountains every chance they got. One of their favorite places for climbing was Mount Richthofen, a thirteen thousand foot peak located just west of the Rocky Mountain National Park. It was early August and the boys knew that school would be starting soon. Once that happened, they would be restricted to making their climbs only on the weekends. They intended to get in as much climbing as they could before that time.

On a clear Friday morning they arrived at the base of the mountain. They had scaled Richthofen before, but this old mountain always offered a challenge to the boys. To make it more interesting they always chose a different avenue of approach.

Breaking out their gear from the back of Earl's Ford Bronco, they started up the precarious slopes, not with the dread many of us would have, but rather, like excited children getting ready for a great adventure. "Ready?" asked Earl.

"You bet!" said Ted. "Let's hit it."

The two boys started up the mountain early that morning, traversing a few fissures with ease and scaling a sheer cliff that went straight up for a hundred feet. By noon they were about at the half-way point. So far it had been a fairly easy climb requiring only a few skilled maneuvers. But farther up it would begin to get harder and they knew it. A quick snack of granola bars and a small bottle of orange juice gave them renewed energy and soon they were back on the ropes making their way up the mountain. The higher they went the more beautiful the view became. It was so quiet and peaceful. That was one of the things that both boys enjoyed about the sport.

By 3:00 P.M. the boys took another break. They were nearing the top, only about another four thousand feet to go. They'd rest at this level for a while before beginning their final assault on the crest of the mountain. Because the air is pretty thin at nine thousand feet, Earl began to yawn. The exercise of the steady climbing and the cool air combined had left him overly tired. Within a few minutes he was dozing off.

Ted finished a candy bar and seeing Earl was

catching a quick nap, decided that they still had plenty of time. There was no reason to wake Earl just yet. Stretching, Ted stood up quietly and walked along the edge of the small cliff shelf they were resting on. The view was magnificent. To the northeast he could see Fort Collins and Horsetooth Reservoir. He was about to return to wake up Earl when the glitter off an object just beyond the shelf caught his eye. It shimmered in the afternoon sunlight. Curious, Ted eased himself around an outcropping on the shelf and over to a new landing just below. The object was just about within his reach when a sudden gust of wind shot around the shelf with such force that it blew Ted sideways. His feet became tangled in a pile of smaller rocks and he fell. Before he knew it, Ted was over the edge of the shelf and hanging on by his fingertips. Below him was a sheer drop of over eight hundred feet.

"Oh, God!" he cried. "Earl! Earl, for God's sakes wake up! Earl, help me!"

But Ted had gone around the boulder and down, and with the powerful howling of the sudden wind, his cry for help was muffled. To make matters worse, Earl was now in a deep sleep, unaware of his friend's dilemma.

Ted's breath was coming in short gasps now as fear began to set in and Ted realized he could die in the next few minutes. "Oh, sweet Jesus, please help." Ted's fingers began to cramp. Desperately he dug at the side of the cliff with the toes of his boots, trying to find a foothold, a crack in the rocks, anything to take the strain off his fingers, which were all that were supporting his weight.

"God, please. I've never asked for much in my short life. Please, won't you please help me?" uttered the frightened boy. Feeling his fingers beginning to slip, Ted knew the end was near. He couldn't hold on much longer. Closing his eyes, he began to utter the Lord's Prayer, the only one he knew.

Suddenly, in the middle of his prayer, Ted felt two strong hands grip his wrists and a calm voice from above him said, "Hold on, boy. I've got you. You're not going to fall."

Ted looked up through tear stained eyes to see a young boy only a few years older than himself smiling down at him. "It's all right, Ted. I have you now. Just let me do all the work." Then, almost effortlessly, the boy pulled Ted up and onto the level ground of the shelf.

Gasping, Ted looked again at his benefactor. It was then that he noticed the boy was not dressed for the mountains. He wore a light shirt, slacks, and a pair of regular street shoes. Nothing about him seem to fit where he was. "I thought I was going to die," said Ted between breaths.

"I know," said the stranger. "I heard you praying. Are you all right now?"

"Yes . . . yes, I think so. But who are you and how'd you get up here?" asked the still-dazed boy.

"I have to go now" was the strange boy's reply. "You really should be more careful if you're going to keep doing this, Ted." With that, the boy turned and began making his way around the edge of the shelf.

"Wait!" yelled Ted. "Who are you?" He screamed.

"Well that's a fine howdy-do," said a voice from above Ted. It was Earl. He was awake and standing on the shelf just above Ted looking down. "After all these years you get a little altitude crazy and don't even know your best friend."

Confused, Ted asked, "Did you see him, Earl? Did you see the guy that saved my life?"

Earl's laughter stopped and his face took on a concerned look. "Are you all right, Ted? What happened here? What are you talking about? There's nobody up here but you and me."

Earl waited for some answers but Ted was simply set staring out into space. This prompted Earl to say, "Hey, Ted. Maybe we better head back down. You don't look too good."

Ted Monroe quickly agreed. He'd had all the excitement he could handle for one day and a memory that would last a lifetime.

CONNECTICUT

A Leader of the Blind

EDIE CHARLES WAS eighty-five years old and a long time resident of East Hartford, Connecticut. In her prime she had raised seven boys and four daughters, but now age and near-blindness had slowed her considerably in these later years. Her children had tried one after another to get her to give up the big, old house outside town and move in with one of them. They worried about her staying so far out of town with only a live-in housekeeper to watch over her. But Mother Charles wouldn't hear of it. The old house had been good enough for her and her deceased husband of sixty years to raise eleven children and it was still good enough for her.

One afternoon, while Katie, the housekeeper, was in town doing the shopping, Edie made her way to the front porch. It was late September and there was already snow on the ground. Standing out on her porch Edie felt the near frigid breeze blowing against her face. It felt good to her. She breathed deeply of the crisp air and squinted her eyes in an attempt to make out the trees that stood in her back yard. There were eleven, one for each child who had been born in this old house. Edie loved those trees just about as much as she loved her kids.

Not totally blind, Edie could still make out shapes and shadows. Easing herself down the back steps, she walked slowly to the first tree and felt its branches. "That'd be Paul's," she whispered to herself. Moving to the next one she said, "And this one is Caroline's."

One by one she located each tree, touched it and whispered a name. By the time she had arrived at the last one, Edie was near the open area that led into the woods behind her property. Thinking of the loving care her husband had used when planting each of the trees, Edie didn't pay attention to where she was going and soon found herself deep in the woods and totally confused as to where she was and which direction she should be going. On top of that, it began to snow again.

Beginning to feel the bitter cold, Edie struggled to find her way back to her own backyard, but the shapes that she saw were unfamiliar to her and soon she began to feel a sense of panic welling up in her. She began to cry silently. Wiping the tears from her eyes she cried, "God, I'm a little lost and I surely could use a little help right now. Won't you please help me?"

The minutes turned into a half hour and the

snow began to come down harder. Still Edie kept trying blindly to find her way out of the woods. She was moving along in a direction away from the house and farther into the woods when she suddenly felt a hand on her shoulder. She stopped instantly. "Who's there?" she asked.

"A friend," said a pleasant young voice. "You appear to be lost. May I help you?"

"Oh, please if you don't mind. I seem to have gotten turned around out here and can't find my way back home," said Edie with relief that drove away her earlier fear. She felt the gentle, but firm hand on her arm again, and the voice told her to come along. He would see that she got home okay.

Within a matter of minutes, the firm hand took hers and placed it on the railing that led up the steps to the back porch. Edie was overjoyed. She knew where she was now. "Oh thank you so much. Won't you come in. My housekeeper should be returning soon and she can fix us some warm tea."

Edie paused, waiting for her benefactor's response, but there was no answer. Squinting her eyes and looking all around her, Edie could see no one. The stranger was gone. Feeling the cold more now, Edie went into the house and the warmth of the fire. She had just begun to relax from her ordeal when Katie came rushing into the parlor all in a huff. "Oh thank God you're here!" cried the housekeeper. "I saw those footprints outside and they were leading off into the woods. It scared me to death. I was afraid you were wandering around out there in the cold."

"I was for a while," said Edie. "I was as lost as a newborn pup. Then a nice young man came along and helped me to the back porch, but for some strange reason, he left without so much as a word."

Edie detected a sudden gasp from Katie, followed by an awkward silence that seem to hang over the parlor. Finally Edie asked, "What's wrong, Katie? What is it?"

There was a second moment of silence, then Katie explained her sudden shock at what Edie had said.

"Miss Charles, when I pulled the car in the garage I saw the footprints leading off in the direction of the woods and since it was a new fallen snow I knew that no one had been out back before I left. I hurried over to the porch and inspected the prints. They were small, so I knew it had to be you. I saw where they went out and where they came back. I was praying that you were in the house when I rushed in and you were. I was so relieved."

"Weren't you the least bit curious about the other footprints—the boy's I mean?" asked Edie.

Again silence fell over the room, then Katie answered, "Well . . . Miss Charles . . . there were no other footprints in the snow . . . only yours."

Walking on Thin Ice

IT WAS THE first freeze of the winter and Tommy Mahan and his brother, Ray, rushed home from school. They changed their clothes, grabbed their ice skates and headed for Turners Pond. By the time they arrived, they found a number of their classmates already on the ice, hockey sticks in hand, pushing the puck around on the ice. To the kids of Dover, Delaware, the only thing better than playing hockey was Christmas morning—and that was great only if you got hockey equipment as a gift.

Within minutes, teams were chosen and the first hockey game of the season was under way. As often happens when kids are having fun, the time passed all too fast and soon it was getting dark. "Come on, Tommy," said Ray, "it's getting late. We got to go."

Everyone but Tommy, Ray, and two other boys had already left. Tommy was trying a two-on-one sweep and so far had had little luck getting the puck by his two opponents. "Just one more try, Ray, then we'll go," said Tommy, who began taking the puck back down to the far end of the ice.

Ray was the oldest and knew they should be leaving but couldn't bring himself to deny his brother one more chance at scoring a goal. "Okay, but hurry up, Tommy. Mom and Dad will be worried if it gets too late."

Tommy raised his stick from the end of the frozen pond and began waving it, signaling that this would be his last attempt. Ray waved back then skated off the ice and began taking off his blades so he could change into his boots. Suddenly, a startling scream rose from the two boys waiting to challenge Tommy. "Tommy! Tommy!" they yelled. "He fell through the ice!"

When Ray looked up he saw them pointing to the end of the pond, Tommy was gone. Ray leaped to his feet—he hadn't taken his skates off yet—and began to scramble toward the end of the pond, followed by the other two boys. As they neared the hole that had suddenly appeared in the ice, they could see Tommy splashing about wildly in an attempt to grab onto the edge of the ice. But it kept breaking away, sending him back into the freezing water. "Ray! Watch it! Don't get too close or you'll go in too," shouted one of the boys.

Ray knew the warning was justified. Long thin cracks splintered out in all directions from the hole in the broken ice. The least amount of weight could send any would-be rescuer into the icy water with Tommy. "Oh God!" cried Ray as he desperately searched for a safe avenue of approach to help his brother. "Oh Lord, please help us. Please!"

Passing seconds quickly turned into minutes and Tommy became weaker and weaker. His movements diminished as the effects of the freezing water began to take their toll on every part of his shivering body. Each time Tommy's freezing fingers lost their grip on the edges of the ice, the young boy would slip into the water which quickly went over his head. Then Tommy would bob back to the surface, struggling for air and grabbing in desperation for the edge of the ice again. Ray realized that his brother was growing weaker and weaker with each dunking. Soon Tommy wouldn't have the strength to bring himself back to the surface and he would drown.

Ray yelled for one of the boys to go for help, then told the other one to find a tree limb or anything they could use to push to Tommy. If he could reach it they could pull him out.

"Hang on Tommy!" yelled Ray. "We're working on it. We'll have you out soon. Don't give up, little brother. I'm here."

Tommy was no longer struggling in the water. He had gone frighteningly still. "Tommy! Tommy, can you hear me?" shouted Ray. There was no answer. "Oh, God, please! Tell me what to do?" begged Ray. "What can I do? Please God?" asked Ray as tears filled his eyes.

Ray turned to see what was taking the other boy so long to find a limb and was startled to see a young man in his mid-twenties come walking out of the woods and straight onto the ice. The man had no skates on, but yet he walked across the slippery ice as if he were walking along a sidewalk in July.

Ray rose to his feet as the stranger approached. The boy knew practically everyone who lived around this area, but he had never seen this man before. "Move back, Ray," he said calmly, "the ice is beginning to crack where you are standing."

"But my brother," protested Ray.

"Don't worry. I will get him, but you will have to move back. It is not safe for you here."

The man's voice was soft, but firm. Ray reluctantly moved back a safe distance. The other boy joined him. The limb he had found would have been too short to have done much good. In silence, the two boys watched as the stranger gently knelt down, then slowly went down on his stomach and began to inch his way toward Tommy. Ray shook his head and told his friend, "It'll never work. He'll go through the ice. He weighs more then we do together and we couldn't even get close. He'll break through, you watch."

"You better pray that you're wrong, Ray," whispered his friend. "Tommy's been in there a long time and it's getting dark."

Ray suddenly began to utter the Lord's Prayer. His friend took Ray's hand and joined him as they watched the stranger inch closer to the hole in the ice.

Amazingly, the grown man seemed to glide over the cracked surface as if he were weightless. Within seconds he was at the hole. Tommy was obviously unconscious. The man grabbed the back of Tommy's jacket and almost effortlessly plucked the boy out of the freezing water. Even with this added weight, the ice did not break. The man pulled Tommy off the fractured ice and to a safe spot where Ray and his friend rushed up to help him.

Concern registered on the faces of both young boys as they watched the man rub Tommy's face and hands with his own big hands. "He'll be all right, Ray," said the man. "Just keep rubbing his hands and face like this. I have to go now."

The boys dropped down on their knees and continued rubbing as instructed. "What's your name?" asked Ray. "You saved my brother's life. My folks will want to know who you are."

The man's answer is still a point of wonder to Ray today. With a smile, the man replied, "They know me well, as do you now."

Within minutes after Tommy's extrication, Ray's parents and a rescue team arrived at the pond. The stranger was gone, having disappeared back into the woods.

You Never Walk Alone

FOR MARY CANTRAL the job she had in Carol City was both a blessing and a burden. As a student at the University of Miami, she found the commute from Coral Gables to Carol City a long and often trying ordeal. But she needed the money and with the steady cutting of federal grants, jobs were not that easy to find. The job didn't pay a lot but the work helped supplement her meager income. Her mode of transportation was not the best, a 1980 Ford pickup with discolored paint, rust spots, and an odometer that had over two hundred thousand miles on it, but somehow, the old battered truck kept on running, that is, until this one particular night.

Mary was tired and it was well after midnight. She was less than five miles from her small apartment and the comfort of her soft bed. It was Thursday—her first class was not until 11:00 A.M., thank God. She could finally catch up on some much-needed sleep. As she sat at a stop light a light rain began to fall and she noticed that traffic seemed unusually light for this time of night. So much the better she thought, fewer cars to slow my progress to that nice soft bed.

The light changed and Mary pushed down on the gas. The truck moved through the intersection, then suddenly began a lurching motion. "Oh what now?" sighed Mary. Her eyes quickly checked the gas gauge—the tank was half-full. The truck lurched again, then almost died. Pushing the gearshift into neutral, she pumped her foot on the gas pedal in an attempt to keep the truck running. For a moment it seemed to work, the engine sounded fine, but when she dropped it back into gear the truck suddenly lurched a final time and the engine died.

Coasting the truck off the side of the road, Mary got out and raised the hood. Coming from a family of four boys, and she the only girl, she had grown up with brothers whose only conversation it seemed had been about cars and engines. Realizing that the actions of the truck indicated a fuel problem, she made all the normal checks she had watched her brothers go through countless times with their own cars. Making a few adjustments, she tried to start the truck again, but it still wouldn't start. She tried again, but nothing happened. What was she going to do now? There were hardly any cars moving on the street and her attempts to get the few that had come by to stop had proved unsuccessful. This was Miami, a great resort city, but not a place you wanted to be wandering around or picking up hitchhikers after midnight.

That thought began to worry Mary. She recognized the area she was in—not one of the safest to say the least. But she couldn't just sit there all night and there was no one she could call. Then she remembered that there was a bus stop about a mile up the street and buses came by about every hour. A few of those made the run to Coral Gables and the vicinity of the university. Closing the hood, she locked up the truck and began to walk the mile to the bus stop.

There was still a light rain and, as she walked, Mary began to notice how dark parts of the street were. The street lights had burnt out or the lamps shattered by rock-throwing kids. For the first time she began to feel a little frightened. It was now after 1:00 A.M. and here she was, a lone woman, walking down a half-lit street on the outskirts of Miami. Every sound seemed to be amplified and every shadow a threat. To ease her nervousness, Mary remembered her mother's favorite saying: "Whenever you're scared or feel alone, you'll always find comfort speaking to the Lord."

Now seem the perfect time to put mother's words to the test. "Oh Lord," whispered Mary as she kept up a steady pace along the sidewalk. "I am frightened and alone. I ask that you watch over and protect me as I travel this mile of uncertainty. Keep me from harm, oh Lord. This I ask in God's name. Amen."

Mary was pleasantly surprised to find that

these simple words gave her a safe, reassured feeling. The tension that had knotted every part of her body when she had begun this walk suddenly eased and she now moved along the sidewalk as if she were out on a casual stroll down main street in her home town.

Less than a hundred yards from the bus stop, Mary felt another presence near her. Out of the corner of her eye she saw someone moving near the alleyway just ahead of her. They were taking great pains to stay in the shadows. Her heart jumped.

"Oh, God, we are almost there. Please, be with me in my time of need. Grant me your holy protection."

Mary struggled to remain calm as she neared the bus stop. From her left, two rough-looking men appeared from the shadows, but they didn't approach her. They simply stood silently watching her from a distance.

Suddenly, out of nowhere, three police cars appeared and a swarm of officers surrounded the two men. The officers had their guns drawn and shouted for the two men to lay down on the ground. Immediately, three officers rushed forward and handcuffed the two men, pulled them up onto their feet and placed them in a police car.

Mary had been watching this sudden series of events intently. Two young officers walked over to her. One of them said, "Miss, you know you really shouldn't be out this late by yourself. This is a pretty dangerous area."

Mary explained the problem she'd had with her truck, then asked about the men that had been arrested. She was shocked to discover that both men were wanted for robbery, rape, and assault with a deadly weapon. They openly admitted that they had been stalking her ever since she had abandoned her truck. One of the officers removed a pen and a notepad from his shirt pocket. "Miss, you witnessed the arrest, could I have your name and address please?"

"Why do you need that?" asked Mary.

The officer shook his head and smiled. "Oh, they always seem to claim police brutality by the time we get to the station. Having witnesses to the arrest is just a precaution."

"I see," said Mary as she proceeded to give the officer her name and address.

"And what about the man that was with you? Did he happen to see the arrest before he left?" asked the officer.

Mary stared at the officer for a moment. Confusion clearly expressed on her face, she asked, "What . . . what man?"

The officers glanced at one another then to the girl. "When we asked the two suspects why they hadn't attacked you before now, they said they were waiting to see if the big man that was walking with you left. Could I have his name please?"

Mary was stunned. There had never been anyone walking with her—not anyone she could see. It was only then that she realized that her mother had been right. One is never alone when he or she talks with God.

Faith Rewarded

JOHN ROBERTS, OWNER and operator of Roberts
Construction Company, is convinced that it was
his guardian angel that saved his life one warm
day in August 1992.

John had woke up that day feeling great. He
greeted his wife with a kiss at the breakfast table
and a comment about how wonderful it was to
be alive. The couple discussed their plans for the
day and agreed to meet for lunch at their favorite
restaurant, something they hadn't done in a long
time.

John's wife, Marie, was overjoyed to see John
in such a good mood. Only the week before he
had been totally depressed over the loss of a contract job that had fallen through only days before
his company was to have begun work on the
project. Financially, it was a staggering blow to
John, whose emotions only a week ago had run
the gamut from anger and rage, to self-pity and
depression, and finally to a round of excessive
drinking.

Realizing the seriousness of her husband's

problem, Marie, through a week of persistence, had finally convinced John to go with her to see the pastor of their church. John's business had grown so rapidly that along the way the church had lost its importance to the fast rising businessman. There hadn't been time for God—not with all the money that was out there to be made, even if it meant working Sundays, which John had done now for over a year.

John was skeptical about going, but if it would shut up Marie for a while, he'd go along. But what could a clergyman do about the loss of a five-hundred-thousand dollar deal?

The pastor welcomed them to his office that night and the three discussed not only the problems of the last week, but the direction John's life had been taking for the last year. Surprisingly, John Roberts began to realize that much of what the pastor and his wife were saying was totally correct. He had begun to allow money and fame to overwhelm his life, placing it above his wife, their children, and even God and the church. This realization was more than John could take. Breaking down, he wept, asking his wife's forgiveness and that of God.

By the time the Robertses left the church that night, John had gained an entirely new outlook not only on the lost contract, but on his direction in life as well. That meeting only the night before accounted for John's new found energy and beaming smile on this morning. For the first time in his life, worry about money and material things took a backseat to his new found feeling and understanding of God, life, and a deep appreciation of all things around him. It was a great feeling and John Roberts felt as though he had been reborn—and in a way, he had.

Driving to work that morning was the very first time John could remember actually enjoying the ten-mile trek he made into the city each day. The usual irritations, people changing lanes without signaling, going too slow, going too fast, cutting him off—none of these things any longer bothered John Roberts. They were simply part of everyday life. On the radio, the announcer commented on what a great day it was in Tampa Bay. Exactly right, thought John as he said, "God, why have I been away from you for so long? It won't happen again—I can promise you that."

Arriving at one of his construction sites, John saw the crew sitting around having coffee. The job foreman immediately went to meet his boss. Expecting the John Roberts of old, the foreman quickly began to explain that the cement trucks hadn't arrived when they were supposed to and that it wasn't his fault the work was stalled until they did show up.

John only smiled and placed his hand on his foreman's shoulder telling him not worry about it, the trucks would be there when they got there. Nothing they could do about that.

Taken back by his boss's calm answer and relaxed attitude, the foreman looked at John strangely for a moment. He didn't know what had happened over the last twenty-four hours, but whatever it was, it was a welcome change from the cursing, ranting, and raving that normally occurred when there was a slowdown in the work. Together, the two men made a survey of the site with John greeting his men with a smile and a joke or two as he inspected their work. Returning to his car, John was satisfied with the work and told his foreman so. Appreciation of the compliment shown clearly in the foreman's face. He would pass it on to the crew.

John bid his foreman good-day and began backing his car out of the job site. As he did so, the first of the cement trucks arrived. Stopping his car, John waited to allow the truck to clear the entrance of the main gate.

Suddenly, a clear and distinct voice came from somewhere in the car. "Quick—get out of the car, John! Hurry!"

Although startled by the sudden voice, something within John Roberts made him react without hesitation. Without even taking the time to shut off the engine, John swung the door open and sprinted away from the vehicle—within seconds of his clearing the car, a five hundred pound cement bucket that had been suspended from a crane and cable, came smashing down on top of the car, crushing it like a matchbox.

Shaken by the near miss and the thought of what could have happened to him, John Roberts sat straight down on the ground and stared in wonder at what had once been his car. The heavy bucket had crushed the roof of the car all the way down to the gas pedal. He would have been crushed like a bug if he had not escaped that car when he did.

The crew had gathered around their boss and the shattered vehicle, staring at both in total amazement at what they had just observed. The foreman knelt down next to him. "Cable broke, Mr. Roberts. Are you all right? Should we call an ambulance?"

Being helped to his feet, John brushed himself off. Regaining his composure and thinking of the warning that had come from nowhere, John smiled. "No, Sam. No ambulance. I think my insurance agent would be more appropriate."

While the crew laughed at their boss's sense of humor over such a near miss, John walked over and put his hand on the crushed roof of the car, then glanced up into the clear blue Tampa sky and whispered, "A deal's a deal. We have a contract for life. Thank you."

An Angel in the Rain

ON A STORMY, pitch-black night in May 1988, Cindy Childs of Atlanta, Georgia, found herself lost and frightened on a back road to nowhere outside Macon. Beside her, clutching tightly to each other were Cindy's two daughters, Carrie, age ten, and Tracy, age thirteen.

It was a terrible storm. Driving rain overwhelmed the windshield wipers of her small car. Brilliant flashes of lightning danced across the sky, at times so bright that it was almost blinding. Each time it flashed and the thunder rolled, the children would scream and press themselves closer to their mother.

Unfamiliar with the area, Cindy had been watching carefully for her exit off the Interstate that would take her to Robbins Air Force Base, where she planned to visit her sister and her new husband. Watching the signs and the mile markers along the way, Cindy had not become overly concerned about the threatening clouds that loomed low and dark only a few miles ahead of her. Realizing that her turn would be coming up soon, she switched over into the right lane. Then the rain came. Not a light sprinkle or a mild summer shower, but rather, a torrent of rain, much like the monsoons of southeast Asia.

Cindy wasn't certain what she had been doing at that critical moment when she missed her turn off. It could have happened when she looked down to increase the speed of her wipers, or when she glanced away for a moment to give a word of reassurance that everything was fine to her two daughters—but miss the turn, she did.

Believing the next exit to be hers, but unable to read the signs due to the downpour, Cindy had left the interstate and slowly continued on her way. Soon she found herself on a bumpy and somewhat perilous secondary road that was taking her farther and farther away from the main highway. The lightning flashed, the thunder rolled, and worst of all nighttime began to close in around them.

Wandering about lost for over fifteen miles, Cindy suddenly realized that she had not seen another single car or truck on the road she was traveling, nor had she seen the lights of any homes off that road. Where in the world was she? Beside her, the children were trying to remain as brave as possible but Cindy could see they were scared. They knew something was terribly wrong. They could see the concern in their mother's face.

"This is ridiculous," said Cindy to herself. "If I'm so sure I'm lost then why am I still going the wrong way? All I have to do is turn around. I know the interstate is back behind me some-where."

Slowing the car in the middle of the road, she brought it to a stop and turned on her hazard lights. The gesture almost brought a laugh from the thirty-two-year-old mother. She could hear her husband giving one of his lectures. "Always put on your hazard lights when you stop on the side or in a road." Considering they hadn't seen another living soul in the last thirty minutes, Cindy would welcome the blaring horn of an an-gry motorist protesting her blocking the center of the road.

The rain was still coming down, but not as hard. Cindy couldn't see any lanes ahead of her where she could safely turn around. Glancing off the sides of the road she saw raging water racing along wide ditches that flanked either side of the dirt road. She had to turn the car around, but was there enough room to do it from where she was? Telling the kids to be perfectly still and not to worry, Cindy opened her door and stepped out into the rain. Moving to the front of the car she estimated the width of the road to be almost twice the length of her car. If she moved over to the right edge, then began a series of forward and reverse movements, cutting her wheels each time, she should be able to make it.

Returning to the car Cindy asked the girls to

remain perfectly quiet. She was going to try and turn the car around.

"Mama, are we going to die?" asked Carrie, her little eyes filled with tears.

Cindy hugged her two girls close to her and whispered, "Oh no, darling. We've just got to turn around and go back the way we came, that's all. Now don't you worry, okay."

Tracy hugged her sister. "Mama's right, Carrie. Remember how Grandma always says we all have angels to watch over us when we are in trouble. Well, we're in trouble so there must be angels watching us from somewhere, isn't that right, Mama?"

Cindy almost cried. "That's right, honey. And you know Grandma is always right about those things. They're probably watching us right now like Tracy says."

Their fear forgotten for the moment, the two girls began to stare out the window in search of their angels. Now that the kids were temporarily occupied, Cindy began to ease the car to the right edge of the road. The rain made it difficult to judge her distance. Her heart pounded and her hands were sweating. If she misjudged the edge of the road, the car could go sliding off into the rushing water of the ditches on either side and there was no way of knowing how deep that water was.

"Oh, Lord, please guide my hands. We are in need of your protectors now. In God's name we ask. Amen." Her short prayer said, Cindy began to ease the car to the left, turning the wheels as hard as she could. When she stopped, the front of the vehicle was only a few feet from the edge of the left ditch. So far, so good. Easing it into reverse, Cindy cut the wheels back to the right and began backing up. She couldn't see the ditch in her rearview mirror because of the rain. She could only judge it by watching the road out her side window. When she thought she was close enough she would stop. It seemed simple enough, but Cindy was not as good at guessing distance as she thought.

Suddenly she felt the back of the car drop and the terrible sound of rock and gravel scraping metal as the frame began to slide off the road and toward the ditch. The front of the car rose into the air and the girls screamed. "Oh, my God," cried Cindy who released the wheel and grabbed her two daughters, and with her eyes closed, clutching them too her as she waited for the inevitable to happen.

"Mama!" shouted Tracy in an excited voice. "It's an angel! It's an angel!"

Cindy felt the car begin to tilt back toward the road. When she opened her eyes she was startled to see a young man leaning on the front of the hood, pushing the car back down onto the road. "Cut your wheels to the left and gun the engine," shouted the man. "Hurry!"

Cindy regained control and did as the man said. She could hear the wheels struggling to grab onto something solid. The man stepped up onto the bumper and began to rock the car.

Suddenly, it lurched forward and was again

on solid ground. A feeling of relief swept over Cindy and she began to cry. Wiping the tears from her eyes Cindy looked for their benefactor to thank him, but there was no one there. The rain had slowed to a steady drizzle as Cindy stepped from the car. The man was nowhere to be found. There were no other vehicles on the road in either direction. Where had her rescuer come from? Where had he gone? Still shaken and a little dazed at what had happened, Cindy got back in the car. The maneuver out of the ditch had left the car in the middle of the road, facing the way they had come.

"Mama," asked Carrie, "was that one of the angels Grandma was talking about?"

Cindy smiled and with a glance toward the sky answered, "Yes, darling, it was. And I can't wait to see Grandma's face when we tell her about it."

HAWAII

A Vistor on the Beach

DURING A VACATION in the Hawaiian islands, Matthew Brodrick and his wife, Barbara, were scuba diving off the point at Mokapu Peninsula. Both experienced divers, they had rented a small boat and made the trip that morning, taking along a picnic basket and planning to make a day of it collecting shells and enjoying the beauty of Hawaii.

By mid-afternoon, Barbara had found a number of beautiful turquoise and pink shells that seemed to shimmer in the sunlight. They would make a welcome addition to the shells she and Matt had collected on the many diving trips that they took each year. Laying out the blanket, Barbara prepared their lunch as she waited for Matthew to come up from his dive. They had gone down together less than a half hour earlier and the tanks they had rented held only enough air for one hour. He would be coming up soon—or so she thought.

Matthew felt as though he was in another world. Gliding along the sand and coral forty feet below the surface, he was fascinated by the clarity of the water and the ever-busy activity of the creatures of the sea that seemed to surround him.

As he glanced at his watch he realized it was almost time to head for the surface. Barbara had already gone up and would have their special lunch prepared for him. He didn't want to keep her waiting. Pausing to take a final shot of the colorful coral with his underwater camera, Matthew spied what appeared to be part of an old ship sticking up out of the sand only a short distance away. Lowering his camera, he swam toward the object. Once there, he slowly began to move the sand away from the top of the object. A closer inspection proved him right. It was wood—very old wood. Matt's heart jumped. For as long as he could remember he had fantasized about being the first to discover some long-lost Spanish treasure ship that had gone down in a storm laden with unimaginable amounts of gold and priceless jewels. Maybe, just maybe, this was that ship of his dreams.

With his heart racing, he continued to shift the sands away from his imagined treasure. As with countless thousands before him, Matt was immediately consumed by the gold fever—suddenly any thought of danger disappeared—only the vision of gold and getting his hands on it had any meaning to Matthew Brodrick.

Above, Barbara checked her watch. Where was Matt? If she was right, her husband only had five minutes of air left in his tanks and Matt was not one to cut his diving that close.

Suddenly, a man appeared among the rocks behind her. Strangely, Barbara, although startled at first, did not experience the fear one would expect at having a total stranger suddenly appear on a deserted stretch of beach. The man's eyes were pleasant and non-threatening. His manner did nothing to make the woman feel that there was anything to fear.

"May I help you?" asked Barbara.

The man moved a little closer. His voice was clear and calm as he said, "Barbara, your husband is in trouble. He needs your help, but you must hurry."

Barbara's heart skipped a beat as she turned and stared out into the water, then looked at her watch. Matthew was not there and by her time his tanks should be empty by now. Turning back toward the stranger, Barbara was shocked to see that the man was gone. Looking out to the water had only taken a few seconds. The terrain around the rocks where the man had been standing was wide open for as far as the eye could see, yet, he was nowhere in sight. His words suddenly repeated themselves in Barbara's mind. "You must hurry."

Grabbing her air tank, Barbara didn't bother to put it on. Instead, holding it by the straps she ran straight into the water. Activating the device, she pushed the mouthpiece between her lips and dove under the water. Swimming as never before, she searched frantically for Matthew. Luckily, the clear water provided her with a good field of vision in which to search.

Barbara soon spotted Matthew on the sandy bottom. He appeared to be doubled over in pain. A dissipating stream of bubbles was slowly making its way to the surface, signaling the last of the air left in Matt's tank. Moving quickly, Barbara was soon by her husband's side. His face was wracked with pain. He kept pointing down to his feet which were covered with sand. Removing the mouthpiece from her lips, she passed it to Matt who was now in desperate need of air. Holding her breath, Barbara moved to his feet and saw a small stream of blood coming from his right foot. Brushing the sand aside, Barbara saw the barbed head of a nail sticking through Matt's foot. The nail was attached to an old board wedged in the sand. In effect, it had impaled Matt in the sand.

She used the mouthpiece, then returned it to her husband and examined the board again. Clearing more sand away, Barbara soon realized that it was not a small board, but a rather long one that would take too long to uncover.

Going for more air, she removed Matt's tank from his back. Using the tank as a hammer, she pounded on the board until it broke on one side. Looking up, she could see the pain her hammering was causing Matt but there was no other way. Quickly, she broke away the other side, freeing Matt and helping him to the surface. The nail and the board were still attached to his foot.

Pulling him ashore, Barbara was near tears as she hugged Matt's neck. She told him she was sorry she had hurt him, but that it was better than losing him forever. Matt agreed, then told her to get the tire iron from the jeep. While he held the end of the nail sticking through the top of his foot, Barbara broke the rest of the board away from the barbed nail. Grating his teeth against the pain, Matt then pushed the nail the rest of the way through until finally it came out the top of his foot. Dropping back from exhaustion and pain, Matt fell back on the sand. His dreams of gold and jewels had burst when, in his reckless abandon, he had stepped on the nail, bringing him back to reality.

Tearing her shirt in strips, Barbara wrapped his foot as he said, "It's a good thing you came down when you did. Another couple of minutes without air and I'd have had it. The good Lord must have known I needed help."

Barbara paused from her wrapping for a moment and looked toward the rocks. Then, as if suddenly realizing why she had not been able to find the man that had warned her, she replied, "More than you know, dear."

Angels and Snowplows

DURING THE WINTER of 1987, Ed and Alice Miller found themselves in the midst of a crisis. Their four-year-old son, Mark, was deathly ill. What had started out as a mere cold a few weeks earlier had gradually turned into a severe case of pneumonia. He had a fever that was running at 104 degrees and he kept drifting in and out of consciousness. The nearest hospital was in Boise and that was thirty miles away. That doesn't seem far, but if one of your children is in need of help, that distance can seem like a thousand miles when you are battling both fear for your child and a raging snowstorm that has closed practically every road leading into the city. This was the situation that faced the Millers that cold, blizzard-like November day.

Ed Miller had done everything possible to prepare his vehicle for the thirty-mile trek to Boise. Chains for his truck tires, extra blankets, plenty of hot coffee, and extra emergency road flares. Even with all of these precautions, he knew it was going to be a hazardous journey for his wife and son. Opening the large doors of the barn where he kept his 4x4 truck, Ed stared out at the driving snow and the drifts that had formed along the sides of the road leading from his ranch—some were already nearing seven feet in height. He fired the truck to life, turned on the heater, then paused for a moment of prayer.

"God, my son is in serious trouble. Unless we get him to a hospital he could die. I ask that you watch over and protect us as we travel on this mission of mercy. In God's name. Amen."

Placing the boy on a pile of blankets in the extended cab portion of the truck, Ed and Alice began the journey to save their son's life. For a while everything went well, the huge tires of the 4x4 overcoming the piles of wind-swept snow that covered the two miles of dirt road that led from their ranch to the main highway. Their hopes leaped when they turned onto the main road and found that the snowplows had been working feverishly to keep up with the storm. This portion of the highway was well graded. Ed was overjoyed and soon was making excellent time, covering fifteen miles with little effort or worry.

Then, unexpectedly, the road quickly deteriorated. The snowplow that had provided the easy access to this point was parked on the side of the road. It had broken down and was buried in the snow. Ed stopped and surveyed the road ahead.

The snow was over three feet deep down the center of the highway, with six to seven foot drifts flanking the roadway. Alice fought back the urge to cry as she stared at the mountains of snow that lay in front of them. "God, Ed, what are we going to do?" she asked.

Ed Miller figured he had little choice. Mark was unconscious and sweating from the fever. They were over halfway there. He couldn't stop here and he couldn't go back. He had to reach Boise and the help his son needed. Downshifting the big truck to low gear, he told Alice to pray and eased the vehicle into the deep snow, making sure he kept the truck in the middle of the road—or at least where he thought the middle of the road was supposed to be.

It was slow going, but little by little they were closing in on their objective. Their spirits picked up when they saw part of a sign sticking out of a snowdrift. The sign read BOISE—7 MILES. Mark was awake again. Alice reached back between the seats to tuck the covers in around her son. Suddenly, she heard Ed shout, "Oh, my God!" Then she felt the truck tilt hard to the right, almost throwing her across Ed and the steering wheel. "What happened Ed?" she asked, dazed.

"I'm not sure," he replied, "the road just disappeared, into a big hole." Getting out of the truck, Ed checked the damage. A portion of the highway had collapsed, leaving a four foot hole half the width of the highway. The entire left side of Ed's truck had dropped off into the hole, the frame resting on the edges of the jagged, broken concrete. That was it. They were finished. There was no way Ed could get the truck out of the hole and Boise was still seven, long, freezing miles away. He had no idea what they were going to do. Looking up to the sky, he whispered, "God, I've never asked for much, but I sure could use your help right now. Can you find it in your heart to somehow come to our rescue? Please."

Ed was about to give Alice the bad news, when he heard a sound coming from back up the road. It sounded like a heavy engine. When he looked up he saw the snowplow they had seen earlier off the side of the road. He knew it was the same one because it had a rebel flag waving from its antenna.

Excited, Ed told Alice everything was going to be all right, then ran back to meet the welcome driver of the big truck. He was a young man and smiled as Ed jumped up on the running board to greet him. "Seems as though you have a problem," said the young man.

"More than you know," said Ed. "Can you give me a hand?"

"That's why I'm here," answered the boy, still grinning.

Working together, they fastened a chain to Ed's truck and pulled the vehicle out of the hole. A quick check underneath showed no serious damage and the truck started right up. Next, the man told Ed to follow him, he would clear the road ahead for him all the way to town. Within minutes they were on their way and soon entered the outskirts of the Boise city limits. The snowplow pulled over to the side of the road and the man signaled for Ed to go on. Ed waved his thanks to the driver and hurried Mark to the hospital.

The doctors said they had gotten Mark there just in time. Any longer, and they were not sure the young boy would have survived. Relieved beyond words, Ed gave all the credit to the snowplow driver. Finding a phone, he called the city maintenance office and asked to speak to a supervisor. When the man came on the line, Ed told him what had happened and asked for the driver's name. They owed him so much.

There was a long pause on the line, then the supervisor said, "Well, sir, the truck you're talking about belongs to one of our drivers names Bobby Lee, that's why he has that Rebel flag on his antenna, but I'm afraid he's not here right now. You see . . . Bobby's truck dropped a transmission yesterday morning about seven miles out of town. It's still sitting out there so Bobby went home. He won't be back in till tonight."

The Mysterious Altar Boys

THE FOLLOWING STORY is not as current as most in this book, but rather, dates back to the 1870s. It involved Father Arnold Damien and the Society of Jesus-founded Holy Family Church. Father Damien was highly respected in the city of Chicago. It was through his efforts that an altar-boy society was established in the parish. Here, hundreds of young boys from around the Chicago area were taught the tradition of the Mass and their duties in providing assistance to the priests during such services.

Having served his church well for a number of years, Father Damien went into semi-retirement. His age and extensive worldly traveling had taken its toll on the old priest. Father Damien now only gave mass on special occasions and provided guidance to the younger priests of the Chicago area.

One night the doorbell rang at the rectory

where Father Damien was living. When the porter went to answer the door he found two young boys standing on the steps. They quickly explained that their grandmother was very ill and that she was in need of a priest for they did not expect her to live out the night.

The porter glanced outside and shook his head as he said, "It's too cold and rainy tonight, boys. We'll send a priest in the morning."

Unbeknownst to the porter, Father Damien had heard the bell and was standing a short distance from the door. Overhearing the porter's words he quickly made his presence known and told the two boys, "I'll come at once. Come in and warm yourselves while I go to the church for Holy Communion."

Once they were ready, the two boys led Father Damien through the cold and desolate streets, coming finally to an old house over a mile from the rectory. Pointing to the top of the dilapidated building, the boys told the Father that he would find the old woman in the attic.

Father Damien started toward the building but the boys did not follow. He thought this strange but went on by himself. Climbing the narrow, dark stairway, he found a door at the top of the stairs open. Entering the darkened apartment, he discovered an elderly woman. She was terribly ill, cold, and close to death. Comforting her, Father Damien prepared himself, then anointed her and gave her Holy Communion.

"Father," she whispered as Father Damien completed his blessing, "how did you happen to come here? Only a few in this building knew I was ill, and none of them are Catholic."

Father Damien stared at her strangely for a moment then replied, "Why, your two grandsons came to the rectory for me. I followed them to this building and they showed me where you could be found."

The elderly woman closed her eyes and a peaceful smile crossed her face as she said, "Father, I had two grandsons and they were both altar boys at Holy Family Church . . . but, Father . . . they both died many years ago."

Today, if you are ever in Chicago, you may want to take a trip to the Holy Family Church which still exists. The church is located west of the University of Illinois' Circle Campus on Roosevelt Road. While there, be sure to visit the sanctuary. Located high over the entrance you will see the statues of two acolytes, one on each side, each holding candles and facing one another. They were placed there by Father Damien in honor of what he considered a heavenly visitation one cold, rainy night in Chicago so long ago.

INDIANA

The Stranger on the Road

DRIVING FROM ROCHESTER, Indiana, to Chicago for a business meeting, Harold Clark had a hundred things on his mind. His company was planning to downsize its operations and he had a bad feeling that one of the stores they were going to close would be his. On top of this was the matter of his wife, Tammy. Just two days before his trip she had surprised him with the news that they were going to have their third child. Harold was happy about the news, he loved children, but in the back of his mind loomed the secret about his company's plans. His wife had been so overjoyed by the doctor's call that he had not wanted to worry Tammy by telling her that when he returned from Chicago, he could very well find himself without a business or a job. Needless to say, Harold had a lot on his mind.

Nearing the town of North Juson, Harold figured that it was time to get something to eat.

Maybe eating would take his mind off his worries for awhile. Not wanting to take the time to stop at a conventional restaurant, he selected a fast food drive-thru on the outskirts of town. Ordering two cheeseburgers, fries, and a coke, Harold was quickly back on the road. Perhaps if he got to Chicago early enough he could find out exactly what the meeting was about. If it was about closing a number of stores, then maybe he would have time to lobby a few of the important decision-makers into keeping his open. It was a long shot, but at least worth a try.

An hour farther down the road, Harold suddenly began to experience a series of painful stomach cramps. Soon they became so severe that each attack nearly doubled him over in his seat. Pulling off the side of the road, he got out of his car and tried to walk the pain off, but the cramps processed. Then suddenly he felt a wave of nausea coming over him and he became deathly sick to his stomach. The torturous ordeal lasted for a full five minutes. When it finally ended, Harold was wet with sweat and his face was as red as a beet. "God, what's wrong with me," he uttered, still in pain. "I feel as though I'm going to die." A second wave of nausea struck and Harold was silently wishing he was dead.

Recovering slightly from his second ordeal he managed to get back in the car. The pain had not lessened, in fact, it now seemed worse than before. He started the car then realized that his vision was blurred and his head felt as if it were going to come apart at any moment.

Struggling back out of the car he searched up and down the highway for any signs of an approaching car—there were none in sight. *How odd*, he thought. Then he remembered—he always took a secondary road to Valparasio when going to Chicago because there was less traffic and he could make better time. Another pain gripped him and he fell beside his car. "Oh, God, please make it stop, please! I need help, Lord. Please help me."

The pain had become so severe that Harold did not hear the approach of a man who walked up to him. It was only when the man knelt down beside him and put his hand on his shoulder that Harold realized he was not alone. Looking up, he stared into the caring eyes of a young man who somehow seemed familiar to him. "You appear to be in great pain," said the young man. "Come, I will help you."

Assisting Harold to his feet, the man gently placed him in the car. Harold remembers looking along the road as he was placed in the car, there were no other vehicles on the road, only his. He remembers the man wiping his sweat-covered brow gently and telling him to rest—that everything would be fine. Somewhere along the way Harold drifted off into a restful sleep. When he woke up he was surprised to find himself in a hospital bed in Valparasio. There was a needle in his arm and an IV bottle hanging from a metal pole beside his bed. His throat felt as though it had been scraped with sandpaper.

"Oh, why, Mr. Clark, you're finally awake," said a nurse as she entered his room. "That's a very good sign. How are you feeling?"

"Where am I? What happened to me?" asked Harold, totally confused.

The nurse explained where he was and that he had been overcome by a severe case of food poisoning. Luckily, he had reached the hospital in time for the doctors to pump his stomach. That explained the sandpaper throat.

"Has my wife been notified?" he asked. "She'll be worried."

"She was notified and arrived here a few hours ago. She's out in the hall."

"Hours ago," said Harold, looking out the window and realizing it was nighttime. "Just how long have I been here?"

"About twelve hours," answered the nurse. "I'll send your wife in now."

After the couple had hugged, and he assured her that he was fine, Harold told his wife what had happened. She listened intently, although there were a few moments when she looked at him rather strangely, but said nothing. When he had finished, he asked where the young man was that had taken care of him and brought him to the hospital.

Tammy wasn't sure what to say at first, then, taking his hand in hers she said, "Darling, there was no young man. They found you slumped over the steering wheel of your car in front of the emergency room. You were alone in the car."

Today, Harold Clark still has his business and still uses the same road when driving to Chicago, but he always makes a point of slowing down when he nears a certain spot on that less-traveled road and utters a silent prayer of thanks for the young man who was not there . . .

A Soul Reborn

Scared and sick, Allen Shelton arrived at a recovery center for alcoholics. He had been crying off and on for three days and was an emotional wreck after having awakened in a hospital following a suicide attempt. The center was supposed to be his first step in recovery, but Allen had his doubts.

As he built up his courage, he forced himself to walk inside. Upon entering the hallway he heard a woman reading from the Psalms: "He drew me up from the desolate pit, out of the miry bog, and set my feet upon a rock, making my steps secure."

Allen stood silently in the hall, running the words the woman had read over in his mind. They seemed to strike a spark in the young boy and gave him a sense of hope. One of the staff came out into the hall and welcomed Allen to the center. It was too late to process him that night, but they would do that first thing in the morning. They did, however, have a room ready for him.

Dinner was being served, but Allen was still too shaken by the radical change that had suddenly put him in this place to eat. As soon as he could, he rushed upstairs to his room and crawled into bed. For hours he lay there crying and shaking, hating himself for the terrible things that he had done and the pain and suffering he had caused so many people. At last he turned to a picture of God that hung on the wall over his bed and said, "God, if there is any chance—can you please help me to start over."

After a short time an incredible soft calm penetrated his body, a serenity, as if he were being cradled in large, strong hands. A voiceless presence seemed to fill the room, radiating love and forgiveness. Allen rolled over and glanced at the small travel clock that sat at his bedside. It was exactly two minutes after midnight. From that moment on, Allen knew his life had changed forever. He felt as if in those last few minutes he had been reborn.

In the days and months that followed, Allen applied himself with his every waking moment to beat the curse of alcohol and drugs and renewed his faith in God and the church. He became a role model for many others during his time at the center. When asked by a counselor to what he attributed his sudden change in his life, Allen related the story of that first night at the center and how he had been reborn.

It was not until two years later that Allen realized how true that feeling had been. Having been hired for a very high paying job overseas, Allen needed a copy of his birth certificate to apply for a passport. Not having one, he sent off to the office of records and within a few days received the certificate in the mail.

He opened the envelope and read the document. Tears welled up in his eyes as he stared at the time he had first come into this world: 12:02 A.M.

Today, Allen is happily married and the father of three daughters. His sobriety has lasted for twenty years. He and his family live in Cedar Rapids, Iowa, and are all very active members of their church.

The Night Watcher

BARRY RUDESILL WAS suffering one of the worst asthma attacks that he had in awhile. It became so bad that his mother rushed him to the local hospital, where a doctor gave him a shot and said, "That's about all we can do for him. If he's still having trouble in the morning, bring him back in immediately."

That night, Barry asked his parents if they could make up a bed for him on the living room couch. He was wheezing and gasping so loud Barry knew that if he stayed in his room his brother would never get any sleep.

For most of the night, Barry tossed and turned. He didn't have the strength to get off the couch, so he lay there, listening to the sounds of the night, whispering a prayer for relief from the weariness of the asthma that afflicted him. Finally, his breathing eased and young Barry drifted off to sleep.

When he woke up, his mother was leaning over him, smiling. "Barry, how do you feel?" she asked.

"Fine," he replied, breathing deeply. "No problem, Mom." Then he noticed a chair that had been moved close to his makeshift bed, as if someone had been sitting there.

"Mom, did you or Dad come in here after I went to sleep?" he asked.

"Why no, Barry," said his mother, "we listened for a while but you seemed to be doing better and we were afraid we might wake you if we came into the room."

"But, Mom, when did you move the chair next to the couch?"

His mother shook her head. "We didn't move any chairs, son."

Barry stared at the chair again. "Well, I didn't either! I couldn't have moved anything last night if I'd tried."

Then, as if recalling a dream, Barry remembered the feeling that he'd had just as he was dozing off. The feeling that someone—yes, someone—was sitting at his side watching over him.

The Savior of the Swamp

IN THE SPRING of 1978, seventeen-year-old Jim Wilcox and his twin brother, Floyd, left their hometown of Winnfield, Louisiana, and took a trip down to the town of Crowley, located in Acadia Parish. They planned to stay a few days with their cousin, Ray, and hopefully convince him to take them frog hunting and gator watching in the bayous around White Lake in Vermilion Parish. Although long considered city boys by Ray, the twins figured they were ready to deal with the swamps and waterways of the Louisiana bayous.

Their first day at cousin Ray's was spent meeting kinfolks and friends and eating what seemed like a never ending flow of wonderfully spicy food at every home they visited. By the time they had returned home that night, the boys had convinced their thirty-year-old cousin to take them to the lake. They would leave first thing the next morning. Jim and Floyd both had a hard time sleeping that night, their heads filled with expectations of what the morning would bring.

Bright and early the next day, Ray readied his pickup and a flat bottom boat for the trip to the lake. Jim and Floyd eagerly helped him with the preparations. Soon they were on their way. As they traveled, Ray began running down a list of things to do and not do in the swamps. Chief among these: don't get in the water, don't tamper with any traps you might find, and finally, don't wander off on your own—stay together.

At last they arrived. Like excited children, the boys helped their cousin unload the boat and place their gear aboard. Within a short time they were on their way through the bayous, headed for the lake. They stared in fascination as the boat drifted though towering trees and hanging moss. It was as if they had gone back in time. The place was fascinating and frightening at the same time. The haunting silence that hung over the area only added to the mystique. Ray pointed out a pair of alligators resting in a small clearing a mere fifty feet away. Jim felt his heart leap as he saw a five-foot snake cutting its way through the water behind them, moving across the very spot they had just passed. The sight had a sobering effect on him. This was not only a fascinating place—but a dangerous place as well.

The trio finally reached White Lake. Ray took them to his favorite fishing spot where they quickly began reeling the fish in. The boys were having a great time and were glad they had come. All too soon, it was time to head back. Jim and Floyd tried to convince Ray to stay longer, but the swamp veteran knew better. Even with all his experience, Ray knew the swamps were no place to be lost and wander about at night.

At the halfway point of their return trip, Ray suddenly yelled, "Look out!" When the boys looked back at their cousin, they were startled to see a snake drop out of a tree and into the boat. In a panic, Floyd grabbed one of the oars and swung at the squirming, hissing reptile with all his might. Had he waited, Ray could have removed the snake safely, but instead, he had reached forward at the same instant Floyd swung the oar. The blow caught Ray behind the left ear, knocking him unconscious and causing him to practically fall on top of the snake. Both boys watched in stunned horror as the snake reared back and with lighting-fast speed, struck their cousin's right hand, then slithered over to the side of the boat and back into the water. Floyd was in a panic, ranting and raving. A shaken Jim managed to get his brother under control, then turned to help Ray. The bite was a bad one. Ray's hand was already beginning to swell and Jim couldn't seem to bring him around—he was out cold. Floyd was shaking and there were tears in his eyes as he said, "I didn't mean to hit him, Jim . . . I . . . I . . . was trying to hit the snake. I didn't mean to hit Ray!"

"I know," said Jim, trying desperately to remain calm. "We've got to get help, but where?" Neither boy had any idea where they were or even what direction they should go to get back to the truck.

Searching the terrain around them, Jim saw how hopeless it was—everything looked the same. "Oh, God, which way do we go. Please God, give me some idea—some direction, please!"

Adrift in the swamps, and with Ray's hand becoming worse with each passing minute, both boys knelt in the boat and began to pray. As Jim later stated, "Heaven was the only direction we were sure of—so that's where we looked for help."

As the boys knelt and prayed with their eyes closed, the boat suddenly gave a *thump* and came to rest on the shore. When Jim and Floyd opened their eyes, they were surprised to see what appeared to be an old dilapidated log cabin amid the trees and moss. A tall man dressed in a brown robe much like those worn by a monk, came walking toward them. He spoke with a heavy French accent. "Your friend seems ill. Bring him to my house."

Relieved to see anyone in these swamps, the brothers carried Ray to the cabin. Jim noticed the sign of a large cross cut deeply into the wood above the door as they entered. He expected the room to be dark, but it was anything but dark. It seemed to radiate light as they laid Ray on an old bed across the room.

"Gather only the green moss from the trees and bring it to me," said the man. The boys did as instructed. When they returned, they saw a small bowl on the table. Inside was what appeared to be a dark mud. The man told them how to prepare the strange mud and moss and how to apply it to Ray's hand. At no time did the man touch Ray or the brothers. He simply gave them instructions and observed. When they finished wrapping Ray's hand, Jim turned to ask, "What do we do now?"

The man was nowhere in the room. Rushing outside, both brothers searched for the man, but he was nowhere to be found. Returning to the cabin, Floyd asked, "What do you make of that?"

Jim shook his head. "I have no idea. Maybe he went for some more of this mud. He'll be back soon."

But as the sun faded and night fell over the swamps they realized that the man was not coming back. Ray was sleeping soundly. His fever appeared to have dropped. Soon, the brothers, exhausted both mentally and physically, fell asleep. When they woke up the following morning they were delighted to see Ray sitting up on the bed staring at them.

"God, Ray," said Floyd, "I'm so sorry I hit you. I went crazy when I saw that snake. I'm really sorry."

Ray lightened the moment with a smile and said, "You oughta be playing for the Yankees with a swing like that." This brought a much needed laugh from the brothers. "Where are we?" asked Ray, glancing around at his strange surroundings.

"Some cabin in the swamp. I'm not ashamed to admit, Floyd and I were pretty scared so he started praying. Next thing you know we ran aground here. Some man dressed like a monk showed us how to treat your hand, then he just disappeared. Really strange," said Jim.

Still a little unsteady on his feet, Ray stood and walked outside. He glanced at the cross carved over the door. Rubbing at his chin and with a confused look on his face, he said, "You know, I been coming into these swamps for almost fifteen years now and not once have I ever seen this cabin. Don't see how I could have missed it. I know just about every square inch of this place."

"Well, it sure was a God-send when we needed it, Ray," said Floyd.

"So was that man in the robe," said Jim. "Wonder where he went?"

Ray kept staring at the cross and replied, "To help some other unfortunate soul in trouble, I imagine."

The three stood silently looking at one another for a few minutes, each understanding Ray's meaning. With a joyous feeling of wonder flowing through them, the three returned to their boat and headed for the truck and home.

To this day, Ray has made countless trips back into the swamps around White Lake and has yet to find the cabin in which a stranger saved his life.

Patience and Angel Warnings

ON A COOL morning in mid-October, Marge Harrelson was driving her children to their elementary school. The kids were being their usual, rambunctious selves, but on this particular morning Marge was experiencing a pounding headache that had her uptight and short on patience. From the backseat of the car came "Mom—he's touching my lunch box, again!" It was the high-pitched scream of Marge's seven-year-old daughter, Kristie.

"Did not!" shouted her eight-year-old son, Timothy, with equal volume and enthusiasm.

"That's it!" came the irritated reply from Marge. "Both of you quit bothering each other and I mean right now!"

For all the good the warning did, Marge might as well have been talking to herself.

"He did it again, Mom!" cried Kristie.

Marge tightened her grip on the steering

wheel—so tight, that her knuckles were turning white. "Oh, Lord, give me the strength and patience to endure the next half mile."

"Kristie is a tattletale! Kristie is a tattletale!" chanted Timothy.

"Mom! Make him stop teasing me!" shouted Kristie.

Marge, turning her head, looked into the backseat and began to scold both children. A voice the woman had never heard before suddenly said, "Marge! Stop—quick!"

Momentarily stunned at the forcefulness of the unseen voice, Marge looked quickly back to the front. There was a four-way stop intersection ahead and her stop sign was coming up quick only a few feet ahead. Hitting her brakes with all her might, she brought the car to a sudden and violent stop. Their seatbelts were all that kept the kids from being thrown into the front seat with Marge.

Within seconds after she had stopped the car, an old pickup truck carrying a heavy load of firewood came barreling through the intersection, running the stop sign on her right. The truck veered wildly, first right, then back left, before hitting the side of the curb and overturning on its side, a short distance down the street.

Motorists leaped from their cars and ran to the wreck to aid the injured truck driver, while Marge, still badly shaken by the near miss, held a death grip on her steering wheel and stared blankly out the windshield. There was nothing but absolute silence coming from the back seat now. Seeing one of the motorists coming toward her car, Marge rolled down the window and asked, "Is he all right?"

"Yes," said the man. "A little shook up, but nothing serious." As he spoke, the man noticed the front of Marge's car was resting a couple of feet over the line at the intersection and remarked, "Good thing you stopped when you did—another couple of feet and that guy would have nailed you broadside. With the load he was carrying and at that speed . . . well . . . I don't even like to think about it. The angels must have been with you, lady, that's all I can say."

Marge nodded as the man walked away. "Only a couple of more feet," he'd said. The sudden realization of what could have happened to her and her children sent a chill up her spine, then she began to cry. They could have all been killed. Both kids leaned forward and gently hugged their mother.

"Don't cry, Mommy," said Kristie. "It wasn't your fault. Timmy and me shouldn't have been arguing."

Wiping the tears from her eyes, Marge answered, "Timmy and I, dear."

In her precious little girl voice, Kristie looked at her mother in a funny way and asked, "Were you arguing with Timmy too, Mommy?"

Marge could not help but laugh. Taking a moment to hug both her children, Marge drove them on to school. Returning home, she passed through the intersection again. There was an ambulance, police cars and a wrecker on the scene.

As she waited for an officer to wave her through, Marge thought again of how close they had come to dying.

To this day, Marge Harrelson is convinced that the voice she heard come from out of nowhere that day was that of a guardian angel, who not only saved their lives, but provided Marge with a new understanding of the word patience.

The Holy Wilderness Church

BILL CULVER, A retired Navy chief from the Annapolis area, related to me a story that goes back to the early days following the end of World War Two. A young man in his mid-twenties back then, Bill was as cocky as a number of young military men who had returned from the war filled with a sense of victory and a maturity that they felt went far beyond their years.

One night, Bill and a group of his navy buddies went into town on a weekend pass. They had been cooped up on the navy base for over a month, processing and awaiting orders. This was going to be their first chance to get out and have some fun without the brass watching their every move and they were ready for a good time.

"It was kind of like back in the old days," he said. "Back when the cowboys finished a cattle drive and rode into places like Dodge City and Abilene. It was wild, let me tell you. We had a pocket full of money, a cocky swagger, and a determination to raise some hell."

The party started at a hotel, then moved out onto the strip, where rows of night clubs and bars were doing a booming business thanks to the returning servicemen. It was well past midnight when Bill decided he'd had about all the fun he could handle for one night. He tried to get some of his buddies to return to the hotel with him, but they had caught their second wind and were still going strong. If he wanted to go back to his room, he'd have to go alone.

Feeling the effects of the alcohol and a little unsteady on his feet, Bill managed to make it to the street and tried to flag down a cab—no way could he walk back to the hotel. As a matter of fact, Bill was having a hard time remembering the name of his hotel or his room number. At the moment all he wanted to do was get off the street before the shore patrol came around.

Bill was still trying to flag a cab when a man came up to him and asked where he was going. Bill told him and the man offered to give him a ride. He and a friend were going right by Bill's hotel and they wouldn't mind helping out a returning veteran. Even half-smashed, Bill was no fool. He'd heard rumors about what a rough town Baltimore could be after dark, and the Base Commander had warned them about muggers and ladies of the evening out to rip off the returning servicemen. Bill was about to refuse the offer when two members of the Military Police came around the corner. "Better come along, sailor—unless you want to spend a night in the cooler. Here come the cops.''

Bill knew the guy was right. Public intoxication would get a sailor a night in the brig if he was nailed by the Shore Patrol. Leery, but with no other options, Bill got in the car with the two men and they drove away. The two seemed all right. They kept talking to Bill as they drove along, asking about where he'd been, what ships he'd been on, and where he'd seen combat.

Bill answered their questions for awhile, then began to nod off. He was so tired. All he wanted to do was find his room and get to bed. Before long, he was passed out in the back seat of the car. All Bill can remember about what happened next is that they stopped somewhere. It wasn't in town, but rather, out on a dark country road. He felt himself being lifted out of the car and someone going through his pockets. When he tried to resist, someone hit him over the head with what felt like the Empire State Building and he was knocked unconscious. When he woke up a few hours later, he was bleeding and his money and wallet were gone.

Bill had no idea where he was. All he knew was that it was dark and he was somewhere in the woods surrounded by tall trees. There wasn't a road or a light anywhere and his head was killing him. He could feel the blood on the back of his head and neck. What was he going to do? Where was he? *How stupid of me*, he thought, *survived a world war only to come home and nearly get*

killed outside Baltimore. That thought and the alcohol made him sick—literally.

Bill swears he was deathly ill for over an hour,
commenting that if he had thrown-up one more
time he would have welcomed the Grim Reaper
with open arms. With a majority of the alcohol
now removed from his system, Bill began to
make his way through the woods. His head was
pounding and had started to bleed again. Wandering about in the woods like a lost child, he
searched for any signs of light or civilization—
anywhere that he could get help—but found
none. He began to think he was wandering in
circles. Everything looked the same. Finally, exhausted, in pain and discouraged, he sat down
against a tree and lowered his bloody head into
his hands and prayed, "God, I know I don't deserve any attention after what I've done tonight.
But I can't believe you would have spared my
life in a war, only to leave me out here in these
woods to bleed to death. I need your help, Lord.
I need you to show me the way. Please, I ask in
your name—help me."

Not long after his prayer, Bill began to feel the
pain ease and the bleeding stopped. Surely this
was a sign that God had heard his prayer. Getting to his feet he seemed to be drawn to a certain section of the woods, but he stumbled about
in the dark for nearly an hour, and found no
one—nothing. What a cruel joke, he thought. De-
spair was about to overtake him again, when, out
of the corner of his eye, he caught the flicker of
a light through the trees. His strength renewed,

Bill almost ran through the woods toward the light. Coming out of a stand of trees, he entered into a small clearing. There, before him stood a small church. Atop the building, emitting a radiant yellow glow, was a small cross—Bill's beacon in the night.

Exhausted and feeling dizzy from his run, Bill managed to make it to the door. Beating on the wooden frame with both hands he called out for help, then fainted. When he awoke, he was on a bed inside the church. There was a bandage tied around his head and a Bible on a chair that sat next to the bed. Soon, an elderly man came in with a cup of coffee and gave it to Bill.

"Glad to see you awake," said the old man. "That's a pretty bad bump on your head—it'll need some stitches when they get you to the hospital in town."

"Where am I?" asked Bill.

"The Holy Wilderness Church. I'm Pastor Kimbell. I found you collapsed on my doorstep. I've sent my daughter for help, she'll be back soon. Seeing your uniform, I told her to notify the Navy people too."

"Thank you," said Bill.

"Were you out there long?" asked the old man. "In the woods, I mean."

"For what seemed like an eternity, Pastor. I stumbled around lost and bleeding for hours." Bill paused a moment, then almost laughed. "I even prayed for God's help, but I'm not so sure he had time for me. I kept wandering around for another hour after that—still would be if I hadn't seen the light from your cross on the roof. Guess I don't warrant God's consideration after the way I've been living my life lately."

Bill Culver will never forget the look that came over the pastor's face when he made that remark. It was a combination of surprise and sudden understanding, followed immediately by a smile that went from ear to ear. Leaning forward, he placed his hand on Bill's shoulder. "Nothing could be farther from the truth, my friend. Do you know why my daughter had to go for help? And why we call this the Wilderness Church?"

"No, sir," said Bill politely.

Pastor Kimbell was still smiling as he answered. "We don't have a phone; we don't have running water; we don't have gas; and we don't have electricity. Son, the cross of the Holy Wilderness Church is made of copper."

The S.S. *Deliverance*

FROM THE STATE famous for its tales of witches comes a story that defies explanation—to all, that is, except Robert Middleton of Newburyport, Massachusetts.

It was a brisk fall morning in 1983. Robert and two of his friends from school had planned an early morning fishing trip. With school in session the boys, avid fishermen all, had only the weekends to enjoy their favorite sport and were quick to take advantage of every opportunity to get out on the water and go for the big ones.

However, on this particular morning a heavy fog hung low over the dock area and extended a considerable distance out to sea from the shores of Newburyport. Although the boat they were using belonged to Robert's grandfather and was in excellent condition, each of the boys knew that to proceed into a heavy fog in these waters was an invitation to trouble. More than one experienced sea-captain had ignored the fog and set out from port only to become disoriented and end up shipwrecked on the rocks and jagged reefs before they had the chance to break out into the open sea.

This was the dilemma that faced young Robert and his friends. Did they scratch off the day's fishing because of the fog or take the chance that the fog would lift and begin to burn off with the morning sun? Robert put it to a vote. He was willing to bet the fog would lift and saw no reason to postpone the trip. His two friends were split. One adhered to the rule of waiting it out. The other was just as anxious as Robert to be on their way. In typical Massachusetts fashion the three debated the issue for a full five minutes with the yeas eventually swaying the nay vote over to their side. They would go.

The boys stored their gear and made ready to launch. Robert brought the engine to life and slowly headed the boat out of the bay, surrounded by a thick blanket of damp fog. Although he had been the one arguing the point the hardest for them to go—somewhere in the back of his mind he kept hearing a silent warning—a warning of impending danger. But as with most teenagers, the want often overrides the logic. So it was with Robert. If he took it slow and easy, they'd be all right. Within an hour the sun would burn off the fog and they'd have a great day for fishing—no problem.

Less than a mile out from shore, everything appeared to be going as Robert had said it would. Already the fog was beginning to thin out as the sun began to rise. The other boys began to attend to their gear and make ready for a day of fishing. Robert was about to comment on the wisdom of their decision, when out of nowhere, the blaring of a foghorn broke the silent calm. It seemed to scream at Robert who suddenly realized the warning was coming from the fog bank directly to their front. "Oh, my God!" he shouted, twisting the wheel of his grandfather's boat, first right, then back left. He was confused, he couldn't see and didn't know which way to steer to get out of the way. Again the horn blared—the ship was almost on top of them. "Do something, Robert!" shouted one of his friends.

Robert suddenly remembered the foghorn on his own boat. Quickly he sounded the warning— but it was far too late. The bow of a huge fishing trawler broke through the fog on their left side and was on top of them before they knew it. The sound of terrified boys screaming and wood being shattered and splintered broke the stillness as the trawler cut the small fishing boat in half, spilling Robert and his friends into the water. "Get away from the engines!" shouted Robert blindly, with a dull pain beating inside his head. "Swim away, or the props will get you!"

The heavy droning of the trawler's engines passed within a short distance of Robert, then disappeared into the fog. He could hear an alarm going off aboard the ship. The captain and the crew of the trawler knew they had hit something in the water, but due to the size of the ship they couldn't stop immediately.

"Ahoy!" came a cry from the fog. "Is there anyone out there?"

From somewhere off to his left, Robert heard his friends screaming for help. "Stay where you are. We're putting a lifeboat in the water. We'll be there in a few minutes. Keep yelling every few minutes so we can find you," said a voice from the trawler.

"Thank God," whispered Robert as he bobbed about in the water. At least they knew they were there. But quickly Robert's sense of relief turned to near panic as he wiped his hand across his face. When he brought the hand away it was covered in blood. He suddenly felt weak and dizzy. His arms didn't seem to work right. He was having a difficult time treading water. His panic was justified. Robert had been knocked sideways by the impact, striking his head against the side of the pilot's cabin. He hadn't noticed it sooner due to the adrenaline rush and the excitement, but now, there was steady pain, and a burning sensation each time the salt water lapped up around the back of his head. Robert had a seven inch gash in his head and he was losing blood faster than even he realized. That was why he was getting so tired all of a sudden.

Seconds seemed like hours now as Robert struggled to keep his head above water. He tried to call for help from his friends, but could barely manage a whisper. Soon, his legs tired, then the arms. There was little doubt in the injured boy's mind that he was about to drown. As he fought to stay afloat, he thought of his mother and father and how they would handle word of his death. He remembered his mother's smile and how, when he was young, she would kneel with him to say his prayers. Assuring him each time she tucked him in that he had nothing to fear, for God and his angels watched over all children.

Robert's arms finally gave out. In the distance he could hear the men from the trawler calling out to his friends as they rowed about in the fog trying desperately to find them. But Robert couldn't yell—he was barely conscious by now. With what energy he had remaining, Robert recited the Lord's Prayer, then said, ''God, I know now that it was you that tried to warn me earlier, but I was foolish and I ignored your warning. For that I am truly sorry. I ask only that you save my friends, for it was I that talked them into this—it's not their fault. As for me—if it is my time, then so be it. Let God's will be done.''

Robert's vision began to blur. Closing his eyes, he began to drift off. He could sense his weary body going down beneath the water. His strength gone, he was ready to accept his fate. It was then that the boy felt something strike his hands. Managing to grasp the object with his fingers, he suddenly felt himself being raised back to the surface. The morning air in his face revived him and he opened his eyes to find he was holding onto a floating life preserver. Still in a daze, Robert hung on for dear life until he heard a man's voice yelling, "Here he is! I've found him."

Strong hands pulled the injured boy into the lifeboat. Someone called out that he was going to need medical attention. Robert refused to release the ring he still held in a death grip and the men allowed him to keep it. The trawler's crew had alerted the authorities and soon a Coast Guard boat came alongside and took the boys ashore where they were met by an ambulance and Robert's mother and father.

Still clutching the ring, Robert smiled at his parents. He had thought he would never see them again. His mother was crying. Robert told her, "Don't cry, Mom. I asked God's forgiveness for what I did and that he do with me whatever was his will—and I'm here." This brought another wave of tears from both parents.

At the hospital Robert required forty stitches to close the cut in the back of his head. Later, in his hospital room, Robert was surrounded by his parents and a very understanding grandfather who never once mentioned the loss of his boat. They were soon joined by an officer from the Coast Guard. He had to finish his report on the accident. By the time Robert finished his story, the officer remarked, "You and your two friends were very lucky, son. You could have drowned."

"I know," said Robert. "If the men in the lifeboat hadn't thrown me that ring when they did, I would have been finished for sure. I was already on my way down."

The officer looked confused for a moment.

Quickly thumbing through his reports of the incident, he asked, "I don't find any report of a rescue device being used, other than a lifeboat, in any of my interviews. What ring are you talking about?"

Robert pointed to the life ring that the nurses had placed next to a chair near the wall. "That ring, over there," said Robert. "I thought about keeping it, but you better give it back to the captain of that ship. I know he'll want it back."

The officer picked up the life ring and examined it for a moment, then looked at Robert even more confused than before. "Where'd you get this?" he asked.

"I was sinking and they threw it into the water just as I was going under."

The officer brought the ring to Robert's bedside and shook his head, "I don't think so, son. The name of the ship that hit you, then rescued you and your friends was the *Maiden Lady*—that's not the name on this buoy."

Holding it up for all to see, Robert read the name. It was a ship called the S.S. *Deliverance*—a ship's name that did not exist in any maritime records that could be found.

The Super Angel

BOB LESSNAU HAD grown up in Michigan. Coming from a solid Christian family, he had figured by the age of sixteen that trying to please God was a twenty-four-hour-a-day job that he just couldn't handle. Every time he turned around he seemed to be doing something that according to his parents would offend God. His solution was to put God and religion behind him and move on. That was what Bob did. It was not until after he had served in the Vietnam War that Bob began to re-evaluate his link with God and the church. There had been too many close calls in the war for him to simply blow them off as just plain luck. It was something to think about.

As the years went by, Bob married and soon had three kids and a great job as a telephone repairman. It was during these good times that he remembered his thoughts about God and the church. He did, after all, have much to be thankful for.

He and his wife, Sandy, became members of the Assembly of God church and began to develop a welcome fellowship with other couples within the church. One day, Bob was in his driveway helping a friend fix his car. The car was facing up an incline and Bob was working under the rear of the car with his feet pointed up the incline. His friend had left to purchase the repair parts they would need, leaving Bob alone under the car.

Figuring that he might as well get everything ready for his friend's return, Bob disconnected the drive shaft. What he forgot was that without a drive shaft, the four wheels become freewheeling wheels. Even though the car was in park, it began to roll backward.

Bob, realizing his error, scrambled to get out from under the car. Before he was clear, one of the front wheels caught his foot, pinning him under the car. Pain sent shock waves through his body as the wheel bent the foot toward his shin. The angle of the driveway and the way the wheel had turned when it rolled prevented the car from rolling all the way over his foot, which would have been painful, but at least it would have been quick. This way, he was pinned, with no way to move and having to suffer constant pain.

Alerted by his cries for help, Bob's wife and a woman from next door came running outside. Terrified, his wife told him they would lift the wheel and he could get his foot out, but their efforts only made the situation worse. Due to the angle of the incline, each time they tried to lift the front, the car rolled farther back which in turn placed the weight farther up Bob's leg.

Soon there were other neighbors coming to his aid. They attempted the same method his wife had used, but to no avail. The pain was intensifying with each passing minute. Bob felt as though his leg was being crushed. In pain, he yelled out, "God, please help me!"

From out of nowhere, Bob saw a huge man sprinting toward him. The man ran to the front of the car, then quickly and easily, lifted the entire front of the car off Bob's foot. Bob rolled away, clear of the car, and breathed a sigh of instant relief. The neighbors closed in around Bob. "Are you okay?" asked one.

"Should we take you for X-rays?" asked another.

"No," said Bob, as he moved his foot and ankle around to assure himself that no bones were broken. "I'm fine, thank you," he told his relieved neighbors.

Getting to his feet, he searched the crowd for the big man that had been his savior, but he was nowhere to be seen.

"Sandy, where is the big guy that lifted the car?" Bob asked his wife.

Sandy seemed confused by the question. Bob asked some of his neighbors that were still standing nearby. "Where is the tall guy? You know—the one that came running across the yard."

They stared at him with a strange look for a moment and shook their heads. "There was no one here but us," insisted the neighbors, who would have certainly noticed any stranger that had arrived among them—let alone, lifted an entire car by himself.

Bob apparently was the only one to see the man and he is convinced that it was an angel, because of the timeliness of his arrival, his super strength, and his sudden disappearance.

Guardian of the
Trailer Park

IT WAS NOVEMBER 1987, and typical of a November Minnesota night, it was bitterly cold with the temperature hovering near zero. Three inches of fresh snow had fallen since midnight, adding to the fourteen already there.

Twenty-four-year-old Randy Toliver lived in a trailer park addition outside Minneapolis, and worked in the city as a security guard for a large department store. The job required working various hours and shifts that seemed to change every day. One time it was day work, the next it was night, then midnight to dawn or evening to midnight—a tough schedule, to say the least. Randy's body wasn't sure if he was supposed to be sleeping or what. There was no routine for his body-clock to adjust to.

On one particular night, Randy had just finished his shift and was making his way home. It was 3:00 A.M. and Randy was seriously weighing the pay and benefits of his job against the type of life he had been forced to live. Planning a date or a night out was next to impossible—he was always on call in case someone couldn't make it in. The only friends he had were those he saw at work. He had a few others of course, but seldom had a chance to talk with then. Whom does one call to chat with at three in the morning? Even his neighbors in the trailer park knew little about him or spoke when they saw him, and he had lived there for over three years. Nearing the turn off to his addition, Randy made up his mind. He was in a nothing job, going nowhere, and all in all, felt that his life served no worthwhile purpose. He would give his two weeks' notice the next day and look for another job. One that would give him the chance to live a normal life like his neighbors.

Turning into the trailer park, Randy's 4x4 Jeep was the only vehicle on the road. That wasn't unusual—normal people had been asleep for hours. Randy could see his trailer at the far end of the park. It was the only one with lights still on in the living room. They were timer activated and the only welcome he received after long hours on the job.

"God, I'm sure not going to miss the job," said Randy as he stopped his Jeep in front of his trailer and climbed out into the freezing cold. Standing on the ice covered steps, he fumbled with his keys until he found the one for the front door. Inserting it into the lock, he was about to enter the warmth of his modest home when he heard a voice from somewhere behind him. "Randy! They need your help! Turn around, now!"

Instinct caused the young man to grab for the gun on his hip as he whirled around—but there was no one there. The only footprints in the snow were his leading from the Jeep to the door. He knew he hadn't imagined the words, they were to clear and concise. But there was not a sign of another person anywhere around the darkened trailer park.

"Will, what the—" Then Randy saw it. A long whiff of smoke first, then the flicker of a small flame that seemed to grow in magnitude before his very eyes. A flame that quickly began to spread like wildfire across the top of a trailer three rows up the street. "Oh, God!" shouted Randy.

Leaping off the steps, he broke into a dead run for the burning trailer, shouting as he ran in an attempt to wake his neighbors. Reaching the burning trailer, he began beating on the door. From inside he could hear the cries of a woman and the screams of children. Randy began pulling on the door, but it was locked. The coughing from inside told him the victims were trying to work their way to the door. "Stay low to the floor!" yelled Randy.

The rear of the trailer was a roaring inferno now. Randy could feel the heat against the outside of the door. The lights of the other trailers began coming on. People quickly grabbed their coats and rushed to do whatever they could.

Suddenly, something came flying through a kitchen window and landed in the snow. Flame and smoke erupted out of the opening and a woman began to scream. The sound sent a chill down Randy's back. He renewed his attempts to pull the door open, but if the trailer had nothing else, it had a very good lock on the front door. "Please! Someone help us—please!" came a woman's plea from the burning hell inside.

Randy knew he was running out of time. Pulling the .357 Magnum from his holster, Randy looked to the heavens and prayed, "God, I need your help! Please don't let anyone be near this door and guide my aim."

Randy fired the gun three times, shattering the door lock. Tossing the gun aside, Randy jerked open the door and entered the smoke filled trailer on his hands and knees. Immediately the smoke enveloped him and threatened to choke the life out of him, but Randy was determined not to give up. Searching with his hands, he reached out and felt the fingers of a woman lying on the floor. "God, don't fail me now!" he whispered, as he followed the fingers up to an arm then a shoulder. The woman was unconscious. Grabbing her by the waist, Randy pulled her toward the faint light near the front. Out of breath and with his eyes burning, Randy managed to get the woman to the door and passed her out to waiting neighbors who quickly covered her with a blanket.

"She has two little girls!" shouted someone in

the gathering crowd. "God, don't leave them in there!"

Out of breath, and half blind from the smoke, Randy knew he couldn't abandon the task at hand. Again, he made his way across the floor, which was now becoming hot. Feel was the only guide Randy had available. He couldn't stand to open his eyes. The pain was too intense. "God, please, help me find these kids. And soon, or we're all going to die. I won't leave them in here alone."

As if an instant answer to Randy's prayer, he reached out and felt the thin little arm of one of the girls. A sense of joy leaped through him. It accelerated to a higher plane when he found the other girl lying beside her sister. Gathering both girls under his arms, Randy crawled back to the door and passed the unconscious children out to waiting arms. Once they were clear, Randy tumbled out of the doorway and fell in waiting arms that carried him a short distance away and placed him on the ground. He was gasping for air and still couldn't open his eyes. Someone tossed a blanket over him and rubbed the sweat from his forehead. In the distance he heard the fire trucks arriving. Randy then passed out.

When he came to, he was in an ambulance. A pretty, young emergency medical technician was taking his pulse. "Well, hello there, hero. Glad to see you awake. Your friends out there were really worried about you."

"How are the others?" asked Randy.

"They'll be fine now, thanks to you," said the

woman, with an admiring smile. "It's a good thing for the people that live here, you came home when you did. That fire could have spread to who knows how many trailers before anyone knew what was happening. You saved more than three lives tonight, Mr. Toliver."

There was a knock at the back door of the ambulance. When the EMT opened it, Randy saw his next door neighbor standing there. Reaching inside, he shook Randy's hand and said, "We all want to thank you for what you did, Randy. It's a good feeling knowing that we have our own guardian angel watching over us while we sleep. We're going to have a formal dinner in your honor soon. We'll let you know when. Thanks again, Randy, you did God's work tonight, that's for sure."

The EMT shut the door and the ambulance pulled away. Through the back window, Randy could see all the people that he thought had never knew he existed, waving to him. The neighbor had called him their guardian angel. All this time that he had spent feeling that he was in a nothing job, he had been providing an unspoken sense of security for his neighbors. And what about the voice? Where had it come from? What had made him turn around, rather than getting out of the freezing weather? They were questions that kept racing through Randy's mind as he was driven to the hospital for an examination. The one thing he was certain of was the power of prayer. Without God's help, he could not have accomplished the rescue of the family from their burning home.

When the EMT returned to his side, she asked, "Just what do you do, Mr. Toliver?"

With a sense of pride and a smile, he proudly answered, "I'm a security guard."

MISSISSIPPI

Entertaining a Stranger

WHENEVER ONE HEARS an economic report released by this or that government agency, you will note that the state of Mississippi is always one of those ranked near the very bottom, if not last in the nation. It is not a state known for its wealth or high rate of employment, but it is home to perhaps one of the strongest seats of religion in America. Few residents of Mississippi complain about their way of life, preferring to put their fate in the hands of God. Such is the story of Hank and Shannon Waters.

Hank and Shannon have nine children, four boys and five girls. They range in age from four to thirteen and have always been the joy of Hank and Shannon's lives. Sundays were a special day for the Waters family. They would put on their best clothes and head for church. The children loved the Sunday school classes and the Bible stories. Later, they would join their parents for the day's sermon, always conducting themselves as perfect little ladies and gentlemen. On the way home, the kids would talk about the Bible stories they had heard that day and the ones that would be coming up the following Sunday. What they lacked in material things and money, the Waters family more than made up for with love.

Hank had worked at a mill for years, but when it went under and folded, he had to settle with whatever odd jobs he could find. Some had called him a fool for not going on welfare—with nine kids, he'd get plenty from the government. But Hank was a proud man and the thought of not being able to take care of his family and having to depend on charity had never entered his mind.

One day Hank went into town to do some work on a man's car. He was a good mechanic and the man would pay him twenty dollars. Shannon was never without something to do, so while Hank was gone, she busied herself with washing and folding a mountain-size pile of clothes. The kids were playing out in the yard, the older ones keeping a watchful eye on the younger ones. Before long, Mark, the eldest boy, came to the door and told his mother that a group of women from the church had arrived to visit. Putting her laundry aside, Shannon fixed some lemonade and welcomed the ladies at her table.

The conversation was only a few minutes old when Mark suddenly burst into the house. "Mom, there's a black man coming around to the back door. He wants to talk to you."

The church ladies raised an eyebrow then warned, "Now you be careful Shannon. You never know what can happen these days. Especially ... with ... those people."

"She's right Shannon. Don't give him nothin' otherwise you'll have him and more like him back here beggin' every hour of the day and night," said another.

Shannon was shocked. She thought she knew these women, but by the strange look on her son's face as he listened to them, it was clear she really didn't know them at all.

Going to the back door, Shannon saw an elderly black man with graying hair and soft eyes. "Can I help you?" she asked. She could hear the shuffle of shoes behind her as the other ladies gathered around the door.

"Sorry to bother you ma'am, but my old truck broke down a couple miles back and I'm walking to town. I surely could use some water and a bit of food to take along the way, if you can spare it."

A gasp was clearly audible from the ladies around the door.

"Why of all the nerve!" said one.

"Remember what we said, Shannon," reminded another.

Shannon was now shocked to find herself hesitant to do what she knew was the right thing. She had come under the influence of the group that surrounded her. Rather than getting the water and food, Shannon stood as if her feet were in concrete. Her eyes met those of the old man who had stood silent throughout the exchange of words among the ladies.

He waited a few seconds and when Shannon did nothing, his expression changed to one of almost painful sadness. Silently, he turned and walked away. As the women went back to the table, Shannon felt ashamed of what she had done. Worse was the condemning look she received from her son.

Hurrying to the table she snatched the pitcher of lemonade, a glass, and the remaining cookies. Running out the door she found the man kneeling among the children who had formed a circle around him. Their faces were all aglow. The man was telling them a Bible story.

Filling the glass, she passed it to him. He smiled as he took it and drank the cool liquid, then continued his story. When he had finished the children asked for another, and then another, until it was late in the afternoon. Finally, Shannon came out with a small bag of food and a container of water which she gave to the man. "I'm sorry about the way I acted earlier," she said.

"That is all right. Too often people are influenced by the actions of others. I have seen it many times," he replied. "But, unlike many, you were able to overcome that influence, Mrs. Waters. That speaks highly of you as does the joy your children have in their eyes when they hear the stories of God. You should be very proud."

With that, the man bowed slightly and walked

out across a field. Shannon watched him until he was out of sight. When she went back into the house, she was overcome with an uplifting feeling that she could not explain. That evening, Hank came home with wonderful news. The man whose car he had repaired had a brother that owned a garage and he needed a good mechanic. Hank had the job. He would start on Monday.

Shannon was overjoyed. Then she began to wonder about the man she had met that afternoon and the feeling she had experienced after he had left. Now Hank had this job and suddenly everything was looking brighter for all of them. Could he have possibly had anything to do with all of this?

That night, after the children were all put to bed, Shannon sat on the edge of their bed brushing her hair and telling Hank about the events of that afternoon. When she had finished Hank asked, "Did you say this visitor was an elderly black man?"

"Why, yes, Why?"

"Kind-looking eyes and graying hair?"

Shannon now lowered her brush. "Why, yes, but I didn't tell you that. How did you know?"

Hank leaped out of the bed and frantically searched his pants pockets until he found a piece of paper. Handing it to Shannon he said, "I met such a man walking down the road when I was coming from town. He waved me down and gave me that. He never said a word. When I finished reading it, I looked up and the old guy was gone. I couldn't see him anywhere. What do you make of that?"

Shannon began to cry as she read the short verse from Hebrews 13:2: "Be not forgetful to entertain strangers: for thereby some have entertained angels unawares."

MISSOURI

A Last Farewell

JENIFER NOLAN (not her actual name) is an attractive young model who works in New York, but whose hometown is St. Louis, Missouri. One day in March 1994 she received an emergency phone call from her father. Jenifer's mother had suffered a heart attack and was in critical condition in a St. Louis hospital. The doctors gave her little chance of recovery and suggested that her husband get in touch with any other members of the family if they wish to see her. They gave her less than forty-eight hours to live. Jenifer's father sounded confused and totally lost over the phone. The couple had been married for over forty years, so that was understandable.

Jenifer told her father she would catch the first flight available out of New York and be in St. Louis that night. That seemed to bring a little joy back in her father's voice. He would have her brother, Charles, pick her up at the airport and bring her to the hospital. Jenifer told her father good-bye, then called her agent and told him the bad news. The agent told her not to worry, he would reschedule her appointments for photo shoots and calm the ever-nervous magazine editors.

Jenifer caught a plane out of New York that afternoon and was scheduled to arrive in St. Louis at seven o'clock that evening. During the flight, she thought of her mother. They had always been close and the thought that this might be the last time she saw her brought tears to Jenifer's eyes.

It was then that a terrible thought hit her. What if she didn't make it there in time? What if her mother passed away before she had a chance to look into her eyes and tell her how much she loved her and thank her for all she had done for her? She couldn't shake that thought. Nervous tension gripped her very soul. She drove the flight attendants crazy with questions. Were they on schedule? Were they running behind? If so, why? Could they make up the time? Was the landing time still the same? Were weather conditions all right in Dallas? How about St. Louis? At one point she was certain they would have gladly opened the doors right then and there and pushed her out of the plane somewhere over Ohio. But she didn't care. Something within her—a feeling she could not explain nor understand—seemed to be calling to her to hurry. It frightened her.

Jenifer was a nervous wreck when she arrived

at Dallas International Airport, where she had to transfer to a connecting flight that would take her straight into St. Louis. Apparently the attendants of the New York flight had notified the attendants of the second flight about Jenifer's nervous condition and the circumstances, because shortly after departure from Dallas a stewardess came over and sat down beside her. She had a cellular phone in her hand. Giving it to Jenifer she said, "Your father is on the line. I thought it might help if you talked to him."

Jenifer thanked her. Her father's voice was still sad, but resigned to his fate. Her mother was growing weaker with each passing hour. She was asking for Jenifer and her father kept assuring her mother that she was on her way. The doctors said her condition was deteriorating faster than they had expected. This information did little to comfort Jenifer, who told her father she would see him soon and said goodbye.

Leaning back in her seat, Jenifer closed her eyes and silently prayed. "God, please grant her a little more time. I need to see her. She needs to know that I am there for her like she has been for me so many times in my life. Please, God, just a little more time, please."

As she finished the short prayer, Jenifer still had her eyes closed. Suddenly, her mother's face appeared as if in a dream. She looked radiant and was smiling. All around her were brilliant, glowing figures in white, surrounded by beams of light. She seemed happy. Then Jenifer heard her mother's soft, gentle voice: "I love you, Jenifer. No mother could ever be as proud of a daughter as I am of you. I wanted you to know that. I love you, darling." Her mother seemed to pause for a moment and look away. When she looked back, her mother smiled and said, "They say it's time to go now, darling. Remember always that I love you."

Jenifer jumped as a hand touched her shoulder. Looking up, she saw one of the attendants standing next to her seat. "Sorry to wake you, Ms. Nolan, but we are about to land. Please fasten your seatbelt."

Jenifer looked at her watch. It was 6:50 P.M. Momentarily confused, the young model didn't remember going to sleep. It seemed like only a short time ago that she had been frantic with worry, a nervous, mental basket case. How could she have simply fallen asleep so quickly with all that going on? And the dream—or whatever it was. It seemed so real. Her mother's face; the figures standing around her and the brilliant lights—it all had seemed so real.

Charles was waiting for her. They hugged quickly then raced for the parking area. She asked about their mother. Charles shook his head. When he had left for the airport she was losing strength fast. They had to hurry. Breaking a few traffic laws along the way, Charles had them at the hospital in record time. They hurried to the elevators. As they stepped off on the fourth floor, their father was standing outside the intensive care unit. Neither of them had to ask how their mother was doing—the look on their father's face said it all. She was gone.

Jenifer broke down in her father's strong arms. After a few minutes of uncontrolled crying, the three walked silently to the small chapel at the end of the hall. Sitting quietly for a moment, Charles asked, "When did she go, Dad?"

"Not long after you left for the airport," he said.

"Was she in any pain?" asked Jenifer.

"No, honey. As a matter of fact, just a little before seven she actually seemed to be smiling and her lips were moving, as if . . . as if she were talking to someone."

Jenifer's heart skipped a beat. "Dad," she asked, "exactly what time was it when mom died?"

Her father rubbed at his chin for a moment, then replied, "I believe they pronounced her dead at 6:45, Jenifer. Why would you want to know that?"

Jenifer broke down and cried again. Her father wrapped his arms around her and rocked her as he had when she was a little girl. "Oh, don't cry, baby. I know you wanted to be with her one more time to say good-bye, but you did all you could. I'm sure she would have wanted to see you too, and tell you how much she loved you."

Now it all made sense to Jenifer. The tears she was crying were not tears of sadness, but rather, tears of joy. God did not postpone her mother's time to leave—but his angels did spare her a few moments to say good-bye.

The Night Visitor

FROM THE WIDE open spaces of the state of Montana comes a story from the past. Known for its bitter cold winters and mountainous snow storms that strand modern-day Americans with their 4x4s and snowmobiles for days and sometimes weeks, it is hard to imagine how the early day pioneers of this wild and wooly country managed to survive.

Montana is a sparsely populated state that covers 147,000 square miles and has only a total of 800,000 people. Over sixty percent of these live in or near the bigger cities, leaving a lot of people with their nearest neighbor a mere twenty-five to thirty miles away. In the winter of 1898, the distance was often a lot farther than that.

Doctor Karl Muller had established his practice in Billings around 1895. He was the only doctor for five hundred miles around and his services were always in demand. If it wasn't busted-up bronco riders, it was barroom brawlers, snake bites, frostbite, and the occasional gunshot wound produced by a difference of opinion or an ace dropped from a sleeve. In his three years, the doctor figured he'd seen just about everything—but that was soon to change.

On one particularly bitter cold and rainy night there came a knock on the doctor's door. When he opened the door he found a thin little girl with rain-drenched black hair clinging to her face and her clothes soaked clear to the skin. The flimsy, small coat she wore couldn't have warmed a dog, let alone a person.

Bringing her inside, the doctor took her to the fireplace and removed her coat. "You'll catch a death," he said. "Let me see what I have that you can wear. Warm yourself and I'll be back."

"There isn't time, Doctor," came a soft, almost whisper-like reply. "You must come right away."

"What is it, child? What's wrong?" he asked.

"It's my mother—she's very ill. She needs help soon or she will die. Will you please come with me?"

"But what about you?" asked the doctor. "Surely you can't go back out into this weather like that. Warm yourself first then, when the rain lets up we can go."

The little girl was persistent. "There is not time. She will die before morning without your help. We must go now."

Shaking his head, Doctor Muller told his hired man to hitch up his buggy while he went upstairs for his medical bag. The chilling rain was still coming down as they left the warm comfort of the doctor's home and rode away into the darkness.

Three miles down the road Doctor Muller was physically shaking from the dampness and the bitter cold, but the young girl, still wearing her soaked clothes and the thread-thin coat, did not appear to be affected by the elements. She must be in shock he thought, as they came around a small hill and saw a light glowing from inside a covered wagon. "Is that your wagon?" asked the doctor.

"Yes," said the little girl. "It is bogged down in the mud. My father went for help hours ago, but he must have gotten lost. She is so very ill. Please hurry."

The doctor assured the girl that everything would be all right as he pulled his buggy up along side the wagon and removed his bag. Calling into the wagon so as not to startle the woman with the appearance of a stranger, he climbed inside. The woman was in her late twenties. Her face was covered in sweat, it was clear to see that she was indeed very ill and near death.

Working quickly, Doctor Muller ministered to the woman with all the medical skill available to him. Minutes turned into hours and soon it was daylight. The woman's fever had broken. She was resting comfortably by the time Doctor Muller climbed down from the wagon. The rain had stopped just before dawn, now there was only the cold. As the doctor was placing his bag in the buggy, the woman's husband suddenly appeared. His face looked worn and tired. His clothes were wet, the shirt ripped and torn in a few places. All in all he appeared to have had a bad night of it himself. "Who are you?" he asked threateningly, his hands cradling a rifle.

"Why, I'm Doctor Muller from out of Billings. You must be this woman's husband." Eyeing the rifle which was pointing uncomfortably in his direction the doctor continued, "She's had a rough night of it, but her fever broke and she'll be fine. She just needs to rest a few days."

The husband's eyes darted to the covered wagon then back to the doctor. Relief showing clearly on his dirt-covered face, he dropped the rifle to the ground and began to cry. "Oh, thank God," he sobbed. "I was lost and stumbling about in the darkness all night in search of help, but could find no one. I prayed for God to help me—to help my poor wife. I didn't think he had heard my prayer. But I come back and find you." Stepping forward, the man hugged the old doctor and cried, unashamedly.

Patting him on the back, the doctor told him that if it hadn't been for his daughter braving the elements and being so persistent, he would not have known of their plight and retired for the night.

Stunned, the husband stepped back and stared in a strange way at the old physician. "What are you talking about, doctor?"

Muller went through the details of how he had been summoned to the wagon, then looked about for the little girl. Suddenly, he realized that he had become so involved in saving the woman that he had forgotten about her. He had not seen her again since their arrival at the wagon. Moving to the buggy, he saw the thin coat she had worn laying in the seat. It was still wet. Removing it, he held it out to the husband. "I don't know where she got off to, but here's her coat."

With shaking hands the man took the little coat from the doctor and clutched it to his face and began to cry again. Doctor Muller was baffled by it all. "I know you're overcome, man, but we must find your daughter. She was soaked to the skin in that rain last night. She'll be sick herself soon if we don't get her into some warm, dry clothes. Do you understand what I'm saying, man? Where is she?"

Looking up through tear-filled eyes, the man held the coat tightly to his chest and said, "Doctor, this is her coat all right, but our little raven-haired daughter died two months ago. We buried her alongside the trail in Wyoming."

When the man's wife recovered and heard the story, she was convinced that it was an angel that had brought the doctor to her rescue and told him so. They presented Doctor Muller with the coat as a gift to remember the experience by. He never saw the couple again, nor did he ever find the little girl that had come to him on that rainy night. Moving to San Francisco in 1901, Doctor Muller married and had two daughters of his own. When they were old enough, he told them the story of the thread-thin coat and how he had obtained it. Today that same coat is in the possession of his granddaughter, Susan Muller Thomas of Fort Wayne, Indiana. Mrs. Thomas plans to pass the story and the well-preserved (sealed in plastic) coat on to her daughter.

NEBRASKA

Twisters and Angels

ON A HOT August day in 1985, Randall Meeker and his family left their home in Omaha, and were driving to visit his wife's parents in North Platte, Nebraska. While the children played in the back seat, and his wife read a magazine, Randall kept a steady ear on the weather reports coming over the radio. Off to the west he had noticed a threatening bank of dark, ominous clouds hanging low in the sky and moving in their direction. Weather reports indicated possible severe thunderstorms and heavy rain, but to Randall, these clouds looked as if they held more than just rain. He had lived in Nebraska all his life and had seen more than one tornado spawned by clouds a lot less threatening than the ones he kept watching approach from the west. The heat, the humidity, and the shape of the clouds had all the elements required to produce a twister. Not wanting to worry his family, he kept his concerns to himself.

Ten miles farther down the road, Randall saw the clouds pick up speed and a hot wind began to stir across the highway. His wife now began looking at the clouds. "That doesn't look good, does it, Randy?"

"Not at all," he replied. "Maybe we better find a place to stop for a while."

Now, for those of you that have never driven across the southeastern section of Nebraska, there is one thing you should know. The land is flat and practically deserted, with few towns and only a few homes and ranches situated off the road. It is not a place to have your car break down or to have an accident. The nearest phone may be miles away. Studying the map, Randall's wife informed him that the nearest town was Maxwell, which was still forty miles away. "Well, maybe it'll pass over," he said with a less than encouraging hint of optimism.

A few more miles down the road it began to rain, slowly at first. Then the storm's intensity increased. Next came a wave of hail and a sudden cry from their thirteen-year-old son, Matt.

"Dad! There's a tornado chasing us!"

Randall and his wife turned and looking out the back window saw the tail of a huge twister snaking its way back and forth across the highway. The swirling killer wind was tossing trees, fencing, and telephone poles into the air as if they were mere paper. "Oh, God!" cried his wife, "it's coming right for us, Randy. You've got to outrun it. Oh, God, hurry, Randy."

Randall knew you didn't outrun tornadoes with a car. There were more than a few dead people that would gladly tell you that if they could. Slamming on his brakes, he pulled the car off the road and told everyone to get out of the car and run for the drainage ditch beside the road. They were to lie as flat as possible and cover their heads with their hands.

As they scrambled for the ditch, Randy's wife got their two daughters down in the ditch, Randy took Michael, their youngest, in his arms and followed, yelling for Matt to hurry.

The roar of the approaching twister sounded like a hundred freight trains coming straight down the highway. Randall looked up from the ditch. His heart stopped as he saw Matt still standing in the middle of the road. The boy was frozen with fright and his head was tilted back, his eyes transfixed on the incredible sight of the one-hundred-yard-wide twister coming straight for him. "Matt! Matthew, run!" screamed his father. The boy remained perfectly still, not hearing a word.

Randall prayed, "Oh, God, please help me save my son!"

Leaping up from the ditch, Randall was about to make a desperate run for his son when he was suddenly struck in the back of the head by a flying piece of fence post. The blow sent him to his knees and rolling back into the ditch. A few moments later, the roar became deafening as the edge of the twister passed over the ditch. Within seconds it was past them and moving back out into a field away from the highway. Crying, Randy's wife crawled to her husband's side and cradled his bleeding head. "Where is Matt?" he asked, still dazed. "Is he all right?"

"I don't know! He never made it to the ditch," cried his wife.

Crawling to his feet, Randall came up out of the ditch. Their car was on its side fifty yards down the road and Matt wasn't anywhere to be seen. "Oh, God, no!" uttered Randall as he hurry out into the middle of the road. "Matt! Matt!" he screamed. "Where are you, Matt?"

Randall was beside himself with grief, when suddenly he heard his eldest son's voice. "Wow! That was really something wasn't it, Dad! You see the size of that thing. Wait till I tell the kids in school about this."

Randall, his eyes filled with tears, ran over and hugged Matt tight for a moment, then asked, "Are you all right, son?"

His son looked surprised as he replied, "Why, sure, Dad. Guess I got carried away for a minute there, but I couldn't take my eyes off that thing. If you hadn't pulled me off in that ditch on this side I guess I could have really been racked out by that thing."

Randall's mouth dropped open for a moment. "You think I grabbed you and pulled you into that ditch?"

"Why sure, Dad. You came running right through that wind and rain, grabbed me around the waist, and rolled into that ditch on this side of the road with me. Then you ran back across the highway. Don't you remember?"

Randall walked to the ditch Matt kept referring to. There was no one there. He looked all around. The land was perfectly flat in all directions, but he didn't see anyone. There wasn't another car on the road in either direction, and after being struck by that fence post, there was no way Randall could have done the things his son said he did. Returning to hug his son, Randall smiled toward the clearing sky and knew in his heart that God had answered his prayer. Like the twister, Matt's savior had disappeared with the wind on angel's wings.

The Blue Light

DOCTOR CHARLES KAELIN, JR., of Gaffney, South Carolina, may have been the benefactor of an angel interceding on his behalf in answer to a prayer for help. You be the judge.

The doctor and his family were part of a caravan that was moving down a winding, snow-packed mountain highway near Lake Tahoe, Nevada, when they suddenly found themselves caught in the middle of a blizzard. As the snow began to fall, Doctor Kaelin noticed that his van's windshield wipers were acting erratically. One time they would sweep all the way across the windshield, the next, only halfway. Then the headlights blinked, the radio went dead and the heater stopped. Something was very wrong with his van.

When the lights went totally out, the doctor, out of concern for his family, stopped the vehicle and had his wife and children transfer to another

one of the vehicles in the caravan. Not wanting
to leave his van beside the road in a snowstorm,
Charles Kaelin made the decision to drive the
disabled van down the mountain. With his
driver-side window open, he would occasionally
lean out and wipe the accumulating snow from
his windshield, providing him just enough visi-
bility to continue a little farther down the road.
It was slow going and the blowing snow and
cold air coming in through the side window soon
made the doctor's freezing body and hands ache.

Soon the snow began to come down in waves.
Doctor Kaelin could not keep up with it and was
straining to see the road ahead. Finally, having to
give in to the elements, he pulled onto the shoulder of the road. His van suddenly lurched as a
front wheel bounced off what felt like a boulder.
Bringing the van to a stop, he stepped out of the
vehicle and nearly had a heart attack at what he
saw. The van had not hit anything, but rather, the
front wheel had gone off the road and the van was
hanging precariously over the edge—below lay
what seemed to be a never-ending abyss of white.
Doctor Kaelin had nearly driven straight over the
edge and into certain death.

The caravan had stopped and another driver
came forward. He asked the doctor what he
planned to do. Kaelin knew he couldn't leave the
vehicle in that precarious position. He would
have to try and move it back from the edge.
Nervously, he eased himself back into the van.
"Jesus, I truly need your help," he whispered as

he looked to the other driver for direction and placed the van in reverse.

Suddenly, from out of nowhere, a stunning blue-white light shot straight through the windshield and struck the steering wheel. Doctor Kaelin pressed himself back into the driver's seat as the flashing light seemed to race through the steering column. In that same instant, the radio, lights, windshield wipers, and heater—everything that had been wrong with the vehicle—suddenly came to life and began working as well as they had the day the van had come out of the factory.

Having witnessed this strange occurrence, the other driver stepped to the van window. "Are you all right?" he asked.

A little shaken, but struggling to regain his composure, the doctor assured the man he was fine. Easing down on the gas, Doctor Kaelin slowly backed the van back away from the drop-off and onto the highway. Within a few minutes the caravan was on its way again. At the bottom of the mountain the doctor and his family were reunited. When the story of the blue-white light and what had happened was told, a number of people assured the doctor that it was nothing more than what is often referred to as snow lighting—but you will have a hard time convincing Doctor Charles Kaelin of that theory. For him, the sudden appearance of that mystical light was the answer to a prayer.

The Shadow of the Cross

IN NOVEMBER 1990, Angela Detmore and three of her friends were enjoying their holiday break from Boston College by spending a few days at a beautiful ski resort in upper New Hampshire. They had arrived following three straight days of snow which had left a lustrous white powder on the winding slopes—perfect for skiing. The weather was excellent and the four were looking forward to a welcome break from the rigors of studies and exams.

Of the four, Angela was the most experienced skier. Her friend, Helen, was an accomplished skier as well. The other two, however, Abby and Fran, were from the Midwest and were the novices of the group. The first day was spent working with Fran and Abby, who proved to be quick learners and very fine athletes. By the afternoon of the second day they were skiing as if they had been born and raised in the snowy mountains of

New England. Still, Angela thought it best to keep them on the intermediate slopes for awhile until they had gained a little more experience.

By the fourth day, both Abby and Fran convinced their teachers they were ready for the big time and the big slopes. Although proud of their confidence, Angela was still a little leery about their ability to handle the swift, almost straight-down slopes of this particular resort. She, herself, had experienced a number of precarious falls on these slopes and she was the most experienced of the group. But finally, under friendly coercion, Angela agreed that they would go for the big one, but that they had to be careful. She reminded them that if they got into trouble to fall purposely to stop themselves, that was a lot better than flying downhill out of control. They agreed.

As they took the lift to the top of the mountain, Angela had a premonition of impending danger. She couldn't explain it, but there was something there. She just couldn't put her finger on it. She knew she would have to stay close to her two friends. They were already nervous enough, there was no need to say anything that might add to their silent fears.

Arriving at the top of the slope, Helen agreed to go down with Abby, and Angela would follow a minute later with Fran. Nervous, but filled with excitement, Abby kicked off with Helen behind her. Angela and Fran watched them criss-cross their way the first leg down the slope in perfect form. "You ready, Fran?" asked a smiling Angela.

"As ready as I'll ever be," said Fran.

"Well, let's hit it then."

Fran kicked out and down with Angela immediately behind her. After nearly a hundred yards, Angela was just complimenting herself on her excellence as an instructor, when Fran suddenly began to weave slightly, then mistakenly over-corrected herself and went totally out of control. Her speed was increasing at an alarming rate. Angela poled to catch up with Fran, all the while yelling for her to drop, but Fran couldn't hear her. The girl was terrified and completely out of control.

Angela's heart leaped as she saw Fran break away from the lane and off the course into the rough terrain. There were rocky cliffs and dangerous drop-offs all along the route. She screamed for Fran to drop but to no avail. Suddenly, Fran screamed as she flew off a rocky ledge, the toes of her skis went up and she tumbled through midair, losing one pole and a ski that went cascading out over a cliff. Angela lost sight of her friend, then slid to a stop just inches from the edge of the rocky drop-off. Her heart was pounding as her eyes searched for her friend, but Fran was nowhere to be found. "Oh, my God! Please! Help me find her."

Angela's eyes scanned the blinding snow. In the distance she saw the one ski that had come off. Farther down was the pole, but where was Fran? The snow appeared flat and smooth as if nothing had disturbed it below. "God, please help me!" she begged. "The snow is so deep and she's buried out there somewhere. I have to find her and quick. Please help me?"

At that very moment, a shadow began to move over the smooth surface of the snow, its movement caught Angela's eye. The young woman's heart jumped—the moving shadow was in the form of a cross. She watched it make its way across the snow, then suddenly stop, with the top of the shadow resting at the foot of a pile of brush at the base of some trees. A sudden gust of wind blew against her back as if trying to push her forward. Focusing her eyes against the glare of the snow, Angela saw that the snow had been disturbed near the base of the brush.

Backtracking a few feet, Angela whirled and gaining speed, made the leap off the ledge and skied to the exact spot at the top end of the shadow. As she stopped at that point, the shadow of the cross suddenly disappeared. Tossing her skis off, she began to dig into the hole that had been made in the deep snow behind the brush. After only a few feet, she felt Fran's nylon jacket. Clawing wildly now at the snow, she dug down until she could get a firm hold on the girl and then pulled her out of the snow. Fran was unconscious. Angela rubbed Fran's hands and wiped the wet snow from the girl's face. It didn't appear that Fran was hurt all that badly. A few scratches here and there, but nothing broken.

Within a few minutes, Fran opened her eyes. "Am I dead?" she asked.

Angela smiled at her friend, "No, Franny— you're a little worse for wear, but quite alive, I assure you."

Fran looked at the hole Angela had pulled her from. "God, I could have died in there. Good thing you were right behind me. You saved my life."

Angela shook her head. "I'm not so sure it was me." She then went on to explain how she had lost sight of Fran when she went over the ledge, then told of the sudden appearance of the shadow in the form of a cross that had pointed the way to where she could be found. Fran looked at her friend rather suspiciously. "Oh, come on now, Angela. It must have been a cloud or something."

Again shaking her head, Angela replied, "I'm don't think so, Fran. Look at up there."

Angela was pointing up through the trees. When Fran looked up she was startled to see that it was a clear blue sky—there was not a single cloud anywhere as far as the eye could see.

NEW JERSEY

The Stranger in the Woods

ON DECEMBER 19, 1979, Nelson Sousa and his partner, Ray, were working as construction divers at a bridge site near Somers Point, New Jersey. Snow had begun to fall early that morning and by noon had become so heavy that they had to stop work and call it a day.

As Nelson was making his way to his truck he noticed that his boss's car did not have snow tires. "Hey John," he yelled, "why don't you let me give you a ride home? I don't think you'll make it through this stuff with those tires."

His boss considered for a moment then agreed. As they started to leave, John said, "Wait a minute." He leapt out of the truck and ran over to his car. When he returned he was carrying a dry suit used for diving. It was one John had borrowed a month before. Nelson thought of taking the suit to the on-site trailer where they stored their other equipment but for some unknown reason decided to keep it with him. He normally didn't carry a rubber suit around with him and had not done so in over ten years.

The traffic was a mess and driving was slow as the two made their way to John's house. When they reached the turnoff that would take them to John's, a fire truck raced by them and came to a stop at the end of the block. There was a lot of commotion and a crowd had gathered. As they neared the site, John uttered, "Oh dear God, no!" Ahead was a terrible sight. A frozen pond, an ominous black hole standing out in the very center. Fire trucks with their lights flashing and off to the side of the crowd, a woman weeping.

"Someone's fallen through the ice," said John.

Pulling to the side of the road, Nelson stopped his truck, jumped out, and grabbed the rubber suit that was conveniently available in the back of his truck. Pulling the suit on as he rushed to the site, Nelson approached a grim-faced fireman that was standing near the edge of the ice. "What's happened?" he asked.

The fireman told him that a six-year-old boy had walked out onto the ice and fallen through. "But it's hopeless," he said. "The ice is too thin for us to get out there." They had already tried. Even a ladder laid across the ice didn't work. And the water was so cold that anyone that fell in would be shocked unconscious within minutes.

Nelson finished zipping up his suit and said, "I'll try it. Have someone get me a rope."

Within minutes a rope was fastened around

Nelson's waist and he headed out across the ice. Quickly it broke through under his weight and he began breaking the ice into splintered shards as he pounded at the thin ice with his bare hands. By the time Nelson reached the hole he was already near exhaustion and his hands were covered in blood from the sharp, cutting ice.

It was only after he had reached the hole that he realized he did not have his weight belt with him. Without it to weigh him down it would be hard to swim underwater and search the bottom, but he had to try.

Forcing his body down, Nelson found the water black and cold. About seven feet down he touched bottom, then bobbed back to the surface like a cork. Up and down, up and down, he went frantically searching the black bottom for the body of the young boy. But there was nothing there. Only frigid water and a slick muddy bottom. Where was he?

Gasping, coughing from exhaustion, Nelson broke the surface again and in desperation shouted, "He's not here! I can't find him. Where in God's name is he?"

Looking out across the pond, Nelson's eyes were drawn toward a tall, blond man in a light jacket standing by himself in the snow. He raised his arm and pointed to a spot on the side of the hole opposite Nelson.

Nelson pushed himself to the spot and went down again. This time his foot touched something. Reaching down with his near frozen hands he found the boy's small body. Gripping him tightly, he surged back up to the surface. He clutched the little boy to his chest and looked into his lifeless eyes. The boy's face was as blue as the jacket he was wearing and he was not breathing.

"Pull me back in," yelled Nelson. "Hurry!"

The rope tightened around his waist as the firemen hauled him quickly to the bank. John leapt into the water and passed the lifeless boy out to the medics who were standing by. They rushed him to the ambulance and were gone before Nelson was out of the water. Two policemen helped him to their warm patrol car and gave him a welcome cup of steaming coffee. Nelson asked about the condition of the boy, but no one had any news yet. They wouldn't know anything for sure until they got him to the hospital. Staring out the window, Nelson searched the far bank for the tall, blond man that had given him directions to the boy, but he was nowhere to be found.

John brought Nelson's truck around and the two men went straight to Nelson's house. His wife put on some coffee and got them both some dry clothes while Nelson called the hospital. The boy was in critical condition, but alive, even after all that time under water. The coldness of the water had actually saved his life by slowing down the boy's body functions and reducing his need for oxygen.

Nelson relayed the information to John, who quickly praised his employee for saving the boy's life. Nelson shook his head. "But I didn't know where he was, John. I went down six different times and couldn't find him. It was that big blond guy on the other side of the lake that pointed me in the right direction. If it hadn't been for him I would have never found that boy."

John looked puzzled. "That's the strangest thing, Nelson. You keep talking about some guy on the other side of the pond but"—John scratched his head—"there wasn't anybody on the other side of the pond—I mean anybody."

Nelson was too tired to argue the point. When he went to bed that night he thanked God for having helped him that night and for, in his own way, providing the rubber suit at just the right time.

A few weeks after the rescue, Nelson received the good news that the boy had regained consciousness and was doing fine. There were no signs of brain damage from the extended lack of oxygen. It was the best news Nelson could have had to start the new year. There was only that one thing that still baffled him. Who was the blond man with the light jacket and where did he go? Unable to let it go, Nelson went to every person that he could find that had been there that night, but not a single one had seen a man on the far side of the pond that night. The stranger had appeared only to Nelson Sousa and then vanished without a trace.

An Angel Behind You

FROM LAURA SOWERS of Albuquerque comes a story of a possible angelic visit at a time of crisis.

Laura and her son, Marc, were shopping in a large department store. On the way down to the main floor, Marc hopped onto the escalator. Laura followed. Suddenly, young Marc screamed. His mother had never heard a scream like that in her life. "Mama! My foot!"

Marc's right foot was wedged between the side of the moving step and the escalator's wall. His body was twisted toward his mother. He screamed again. The escalator continued to move downward.

In the panic of the moment, the danger at the bottom of the escalator flashed through Laura's mind—the thought of her son's foot being severed.

"Turn off the escalator!" she screamed as loud as possible. "Somebody help!" Then she cried,

"Oh, dear God, dear God, help us! Help us!"

Several people at the base of the steps began a flurry of activity. The escalator suddenly stopped—someone had pressed an emergency button at the bottom of the steps.

"Thank you, Father," whispered Laura.

A frightened Marc clutched her arm and cried as Laura struggled to get a better look at his trapped foot. A chill raced down her spine when she saw the tiny space in which her son's foot was caught. It looked no more than a quarter of an inch wide. All she could see of his foot was the heel. The rest of the small foot had disappeared into the jaws of the machine.

"Someone call the fire department!" she shouted.

Marc looked up at his mother desperately. "Mama," he said, "pray!"

Laura crouched next to her son and holding him tight, prayed. For a moment he was quiet, then he began to cry again. "Daddy!" he called, "Daddy—I want Daddy!"

Laura shouted out her husband's work number and asked someone to call and tell him the situation. The two of them sat waiting. Marc continued to cry, but there was nothing his mother could do. As the minutes passed, Laura began to see dark images of crutches and wheelchairs. She had always taken it for granted that Marc would grow up playing baseball and soccer, and playing like any other child on strong legs and feet. Now, she wasn't so certain.

Laura's prayers were as scattered as her feelings at that moment, and she searched her memory for a Bible verse to hold on to.

"And we know that all things work together for good to them that love God, to them who are the called according to His purpose" (Romans 8:28). This was one of the few verses that Laura had memorized.

"You promised, Lord!" she cried. "And we know all things . . ."—over and over she said the verse—" . . . called according to His purpose."

Marc looked up at his mother and said, "Mama, my bones feel all broke and bleedy."

Laura clutched his blond head tighter to her, but now it was Laura that was feeling faint. "I can't faint, Lord," she prayed. "Marc needs me—Oh, Lord, I know You are here! But where? Help me!"

At that moment Laura felt warm soft arms enfolding her from behind. A woman's soothing voice said quietly in her ear, "Jesus is here, Jesus is here."

The woman had come down the steps of the escalator and sat on the step above Laura. She gently rocked the worried mother from side to side, surrounding her body with a calm embrace. "Tell your son that his foot is all right," she whispered into Laura's ear. There was a certain assurance in her voice.

"Marc," she said, "Your foot is all right."

"Tell him you'll buy him a pair of new shoes—whatever kind he wants."

"I'll buy you a new pair of shoes. Any kind you want."

Marc's crying stopped and his little face beamed. "Cowboy boots? Like Daddy's?" They were talking about new shoes—shoes for two healthy feet! For the first time since the ordeal had began, Laura felt hope. Maybe, just maybe, his foot really would be all right.

"Tell him there are no broken bones," said the soft voice behind her.

Laura did and Marc smiled for the first time. As if he believed, too.

The firemen arrived. Two men with crowbars pried the step away from the escalator wall, freeing Marc's foot at long last. His shoe was a tattered mess. It took all Laura's courage to watch as the men removed the shredded sock from Marc's foot, and when they did, it was red and bruised, but still a whole foot.

Laura turned to share her joy with her new found friend behind her, but when she turned all she saw was a woman's leg as she turned the corner at the top of the escalator. Laura never did see her face.

Laura's husband arrived a few minutes later, just as the firemen were placing Marc on a stretcher. He was still sobbing, but he could wiggle his toes. At the hospital, Xrays confirmed what Laura already knew—there were no broken bones, only bruises and swelling.

To this day Laura does not know who the woman was who helped her get through that ordeal, or who assured her that Jesus was with them and that he always keeps his promises.

Many people have suggested that the woman was an angel of the Lord. Laura can't be sure about that, but of one thing she is certain: She was heaven-sent.

Silent Acceptance

IRMA LEVESQUE GREW up in rural New Hampshire and was the eldest daughter in a family of six children. In her chaotic household she found refuge in make-believe, often pretending that she was a beautiful girl named Joan Bishop (Joan from Joan of Arc and Bishop from the English translation of her French last name). Irma never told anyone else about Joan Bishop. It was a secret between God and her.

Little girls grow up, though, and the day came when Irma said good-bye to Joan Bishop . . . and to God. She moved to New York, got caught up in a fiercely competitive line of work, and gradually found her personal life getting lonelier and lonelier. In time she knew she wanted to return to God, but hesitated. Would God welcome her back after such a long absence?

One Sunday morning she could not stay away any longer. She went to Grace Church which was close to her apartment. Irma walked down the aisle, past the old pews, each with its own waist-high door and tiny brass nameplate, relics from the past century when parishioners purchased their seats. Irma chose an empty pew and closed the door behind her.

"Please, God," she began, "I'm so lonely and afraid. Are you here? Is this the place for me? Will these people all around me take me in?" Irma wanted God's assurance that she should stay in that church, but no assurance seemed forthcoming. Suddenly, she felt an overpowering urge to leave.

Hastily gathering up her coat and scarf, Irma opened the pew door and stepped into the aisle. As she turned to shut the old fashioned door, her eyes were drawn to the tiny brass nameplate that was attached. The brass read J. BISHOP.

Irma was so overcome that she returned to her pew and continued her prayers—she was home again.

The Night Nurse

SANDRA MICHAELS OF Charlotte, North Carolina, is a marketing assistant who recounts a story from her youth.

The younger of two children, she was raised Catholic. When she was about four years old, her brother came down with a case of the measles. Her family doctor thought it best that Sandra be given an inoculation so that she would have a less severe case than the one which she was certain to get after having such close contact with her brother. The parents agreed and the girl was given the shot. Unfortunately, the inoculation worked in reverse on Sandra and nearly proved fatal to her.

As she lay in bed, she could see the thick blankets covering the windows, and she was aware of a gentle lady in white who sat quietly next to her bed throughout her illness. Sandra assumed that the kind lady was a nurse hired by her parents.

It was almost thirty years later when Sandra was visiting her mother and the subject of her severe bout with the measles and how she had almost died came up. It was the first time Sandra had ever mentioned the kindly nurse her mother had hired to watch over her.

To her surprise, her mother asked what she was talking about. Sandra told of a vivid memory of a woman in white sitting beside her bed throughout the ordeal. Only then did Sandra learn that there had been no nurse or any other person for that matter, sitting next to her during her illness. Sandra and her mother are convinced that her visitor was her guardian angel.

Hands From the Deep

RICHARD DENT OF Bismarck, North Dakota, was spending the summer at home with some of his college friends from the University of Nebraska. Richard's family owned a cattle ranch and the friends had agreed to spend the summer helping out around the ranch in exchange for free room and board, horse back riding, and some of the best biscuits and gravy anywhere in the state. It would almost be like spending the summer on a dude ranch for many of them. Richard's mother seldom allowed her husband to work the boys, saying, "Oh, now Charles, it's their summer break. Let 'em have a little fun will you for goodness sakes."

One morning, Richard and his friends decided it would be a perfect day to go swimming. Lake Oahe was only a short distance to the south and Richard's uncle, who was there to help with some branding, suggested that they take his ski boat along. He didn't mind. There were three sets of skis in the tack shed. Richard and his friends were welcome to use them. The boys were quick to accept the offer and were soon on their way to the lake with the boat. But, like most college kids who feel that they have matured beyond their years, Richard and his friends stopped along the way and bought a case of beer for the cooler. Now they could really have some fun—or so they thought.

They reached the lake by noon and soon had the boat in the water. Everyone seemed to have a beer in his hand and the mood was one of friendly rough-housing and fun. Since the boat belonged to his uncle, Richard was the designated driver. After nearly two hours of pulling skiers around the lake, Richard wanted his turn in the water and told his friend, Walter, to drive the boat for him.

As Richard leapt into the water and began swimming back for the tow rope, Walter opened another beer—his fifth of the afternoon. The other two boys in the boat had drank as much and were paying little attention to Richard at the rear of the boat. Finally ready, Richard yelled to Walter that he was ready.

Walter gunned the engine and the large boat roared away at near breakneck speed, jerking Richard up on his skis amid the wild cheers of his friends in the boat. Everything seemed to be going fine until Walter began cutting the boat in a series of hard right turns. Soon, Richard found himself practically flying around the lake and due to the beer, having a difficult time staying on his skis.

Perhaps it was the effect of the mist spraying up in his face, or the combination of water and wind, but for whatever reason, Richard Dent suddenly became fully alert. It was as if the alcohol had simply vanished from his body. His mind was clear and every muscle in his body tense. There was the feeling of impending danger welling up within him and it frightened the boy. From somewhere around him he heard a voice say, "Drop the rope, Richard! Do it now!"

Instinct and the forcefulness of the voice caused him to react at once. He released the rope and went tumbling across the water for a few seconds as if he were a rock that had been flat-skipped across the lake. When he finally came up for air he saw the tow rope strike something in the water, break, and go flying through the air. Not one of the boys in the boat had even noticed. As far as they knew, Richard was still skiing behind them.

Swimming to the spot where the rope had disintegrated, Richard found what was left of a homemade raft that had been constructed of two old fifty-five gallon barrels and some two-by-fours. The barrels were rusted and had a number of jagged edges sticking out from the sides, and rows of rusty, bent nails adorned the wood. Had he hit this thing at the speed he was going it would have more than likely killed him or at least crippled him for sure. Treading water, he looked along the shores of the bank, there was no one else around. He hadn't even seem the raft. Where had the warning come from? How had he heard it so clearly among the wind and slapping of the skis on the top of the water? "God, I was lucky," he sighed, as he looked again at the jagged metal and rusted nails.

But Richard's troubles were far from over. Walter and the others had suddenly realized that their friend was no longer behind them and were now racing the boat full speed back in Richard's direction to search for him. The only problem was that Walter was running the boat wide open. The bow of the boat rose up out of the water in the front and they had no way of seeing Richard bobbing in the water in front of them.

"Oh, sweet Jesus," shouted Richard. "They're going to run right over me!" Richard tried to swim out of the way of the approaching craft but his arms and legs were tired from treading water for so long. "Oh, God, help me! Please. They don't see me! Help me, Lord!"

The boat was less than fifty yards from the terrified boy and heading straight for him. If the impact didn't kill him the propeller would cut him to pieces. Richard struggled to wave them off. He screamed and yelled, but the boat continued on its deadly course. Fear gripped Richard's stomach. He was as good as dead and he knew it.

Suddenly, he felt something or someone grab his feet and jerk him straight down into the depths of the lake with such force that water burned his nose as it shot up his nostrils. Seconds later he heard the roar of the engines of the ski boat as it passed overhead and saw the whirling bubbles from the spinning propeller blades as they cut through the water behind the boat. As soon as the boat had passed, he felt his feet come free and bobbed back up to the surface. This time one of the boys in the back of the boat saw him and yelled for Walter to slow down and turn around. He thought they surely had hit Richard as they passed over that very spot.

It was a relieved bunch of friends who helped Richard into the boat that afternoon. What had started out as a fun trip had nearly ended in disaster. The boys all learned something that afternoon. Those in the boat learned that alcohol and boating can be as deadly on the water as alcohol and driving can be on the open highway. It had nearly cost them the life of their best friend. And for Richard, the learning experience had been both mentally and spiritually uplifting. He suddenly realized where the earlier warning had come from and that his prayers for help had been answered in a very convincing way by a loving and forgiving God who had sent His angels down to protect him.

OHIO

The White Dog

NEVA JOYCE COIL of rural Toronto, Ohio, tells of
an incident that occurred involving her dog and
an unfamiliar visitor in the woods near her
home.

Neva owned a dog called Skipper, a German
keeshund, that had been blinded at an early age
by a chemical substance sprayed by a nervous
biker whom Skipper had been chasing along the
road. In spite of this handicap, Skipper was a
wonderful companion, a beautiful and smart animal, and an excellent watchdog. He guarded
their home with passion, always seeming to
know if the footsteps of approaching people
were those of family or friends. The family could
tell whether his bark was a friendly greeting or
an ominous warning of a stranger's approach.

It was winter time and Neva was returning
home from a trip into town. The Coils lived outside Toronto on four acres of beautifully wooded

land. They enjoyed the quiet and peace of country living. On this particular day, Neva pulled
her car into the driveway and opened her door.
Bracing herself against the icy blast of wind and
rain, she hurried toward the house. As she made
her way, she happened to glance toward the
Skipper's doghouse when she realized he hadn't
barked when she drove up. She looked again.
Skipper wasn't there! Her heart sank as she
moved to the doghouse for a closer look. Not
only was the dog gone, but he had dragged his
chain along with him. "Why today of all days?"
grumbled Neva to herself. "The coldest day of
the year. If his chain gets caught or tangled in
the brush and he can't pull himself free, he'll
freeze to death before morning."

Beside herself with concern, Neva went into
the house and began digging out some warmer
clothing. She then phoned her daughter, Linda,
who lived in town, and told her what had happened and to let her know that she was going
into the woods to search for Skipper. Linda told
her mother to wait for her and insisted that she
was going with her.

Dressed warmly, Linda arrived and the two
women headed out into the icy rain and the
woods directly behind the house. Suddenly, they
could hear Skipper barking, the sound echoing
down through the hollows. He sounded very
close. But both women knew all too well that
sound carried in the woods and a sound that
seemed to be coming from the north could actually be coming from the south. The ground

was not yet completely frozen. As they moved through the woods they watched for tracks or any sign that might give them a clue as to the true direction Skipper may have gone. They found deer tracks and those of other animals, but no dog prints. Nothing to signify that Skipper had gone in that direction. Linda and her mother remained in the woods until ice began to form on their coats. Satisfied that they were heading the wrong way, they returned to the house to warm themselves before heading out again in another direction.

A quick cup of coffee and they were on their way again, this time going off into the east side of the woods. They found nothing there, and returned to the house. The third time out they headed to the west side. Each time they went out they prayed both aloud and in silence, "Lord, please help us to find him." But soon the weather began to penetrate their very bones and they became more and more discouraged. The idea of giving up occurred to them both at one time or another, but each time the thought of Skipper blind, alone, and facing a frozen death kept them going. Even more frustrating was the fact that they could hear the dog barking off in the distance, but they had no idea where.

Returning to the house one more time, the two determined women warmed themselves for one final try. Darkness was beginning to close in on them and the rain was now turning to sleet. There would no other attempts after this one and they both knew it. Stepping off the back porch, they could hear Skipper barking again. It was a hoarse bark, barely audible now. Neva and Linda began to pray in earnest. "God, please help us find him before dark. He has suffered so much already. Please!"

Reaching the edge of the woods, they paused to decide on a final direction in which to launch their final search. Suddenly, they were startled to see a very large dog they had never seen before come out of the woods. He was a beautiful animal, much like a German police dog, but pure white. He came toward them, then stopped and began wagging his tail. Neva and her daughter stood perfectly still, trying to decide what they should do. While they watched the white dog, he ran a little ways into the woods, then returned to where he had been standing before. A second time he ran into the woods and came back. After the third time, Linda said, "Mother, he wants us to follow him."

Cautiously, the two women followed as the dog ran off into the woods, coming back every so often to make sure the women were still following him. Little by little they seemed to be getting closer to Skipper's weak bark. Soon they rounded a clump of bushes and there stood Skipper. His long fur coat was covered with ice and his chain was tangled in a clump of brush and around the steel leg of an electrical tower. As the two happy women ran toward Skipper, the big white dog moved back as if to say, "Come on, I won't bother you."

Still cautious of the white dog, Neva and Linda

tried to keep an eye on the dog while they worked feverishly to untangle Skipper's chain, but soon the other dog was forgotten. When they finally had Skipper free, they looked around for the white dog; he was nowhere to be found. He had gone out of their lives as mysteriously as he had come.

Linda and her mother often ask themselves if it was a dog or an angel who caused them to see him as a dog, because they would never have followed a stranger into those woods. They feel that they will never know the answer to that question. What they do know is that they had never seen the white dog before, nor have they seen him since—but that once, he came as an answer to a prayer.

The Deadbolt

WHEN MACY KRUPICKA was six years old, her family lived in Oklahoma City. Their neighborhood was not one that abounded with a sense of security. Cruising police cars were a necessity and a frequent sight in the area. For this reason the family always kept the doors locked and bolted at night. To get out the back door of the house, Macy's father had a special key that opened the dead bolt from inside.

One night Macy was awakened suddenly by the sound of rolling thunder, flashing lightning, and a torrential downpour. Frightened by the storm, she ran out of her room and into the hallway, heading for her parents' bedroom. As she rounded the corner of the hall doorway she encountered a thick, billowing cloud of smoke. Bright red-orange flames were coming from the living room. Macy's house had been struck by lightning.

Cut off from her parents, Macy knew she had to get out of the house, but how? She couldn't reach the front door because of the heat and increasing flames, and the back door was locked with a dead bolt—a dead bolt for which she had no key.

On the verge of panic, Macy was suddenly relieved, when in the darkness she felt her father's warm hand leading her down the hall and out the back door to their backyard. As she stepped out into the rain, she felt her father release her hand and when she turned around he was gone. Frightened, she looked back at the house. Glass shattered as the heat broke windows and flames seemed to leap out from inside and climb up the sides of the small home. Tears filled young Macy's eyes and fear gripped her heart. Where was the rest of her family? Suddenly, above the noise of the rain and crackling fire she heard a familiar voice calling her name. "Macy! Macy!" She turned to see her mother standing across the yard calling her name.

"I'm here, Mama!" she yelled, waving and running to her mother, who scooped her up in her arms and hugged her close. "Are you all right, baby?" asked her mother.

"Yes, Mama, I'm all right."

Carrying her little girl, Macy's mother rushed back around to the front of the house where Macy was overjoyed to see her father and her three-year-old sister, Amy. Macy's dad was holding her little baby brother, Kent.

Leaning down and kissing her, Macy's father

said, "You're safe, Macy. Everything's all right now. You're safe."

Looking up at her father, she asked, "Where did you go, Daddy? Why did you leave me in the backyard by myself?"

Her father and mother stared at her for a moment, then her father said, "What do you mean, daughter? I didn't leave you anywhere. When I saw the flames I tried to get to your room but the flames were too high. I couldn't get through the hallway."

"But who led me through the smoke to the back door? And who opened the dead bolt on the back door?"

For the first time, Macy's parents began to realize what their daughter was trying to tell them. Kneeling around the young girl, they hugged her and wept. For now they knew that their daughter's life had been spared by a caring God and an angel who could open dead bolts without a key—a key that was now nothing more than a molten piece of copper in what had been her parents' bedroom.

The Angel of the Wilderness

THE DATE IS May 5, 1864. The place is a dark woodland south of the Rapidan River, ten miles west of Fredericksburg, Pennsylvania. The area is known as the Wilderness, a forbidding woodland consisting of impenetrable, tangled underbrush, dense woods, gullies, streams, and a handful of clearings. There are few roads through the area and most of them are mere wagon tracks. The only good passage around the entanglement and brush is the Orange Turnpike to the north and the Orange Plank Road to the south.

In this wilderness, over five thousand men will lose their lives over the next two days. The wounded will number over fifteen thousand, and the missing will be tallied at over four thousand.

It is a place that will be remembered by Yankees and Rebels alike as hell on Earth.

On the morning of the fifth, Generals Ulysses S. Grant and George Meade were notified that Confederate forces under General Richard Stoddert Ewell were moving on the Orange Turnpike. Thinking the force to be only a division, Grant ordered an attack. Union forces under General Gouverneur Kemble Warren engaged the Confederate force, an encounter that soon escalated into a full-fledged battle. Grant quickly realized that the Confederate troops were not a minor element of General Robert E. Lee's army, but the main force itself.

Because of the thick woods, the men were often firing at one another at point-blank range. Battle lines became confused in the smoke-filled woods; regiments lost contact with one another. Commanders led their men by following the sounds of firing, often finding themselves shooting at each other or at the muzzle flashes of an enemy that they could not see.

To add to the confusion, Confederate General A. P. Hill began to advance up the Orange Plank Road to the south. There he was met by Union General Winfield Scott Hancock, and a separate and equally desperate battle ensued. Again the battle was fought at close quarters, often hand-to-hand, with bayonets and rifles used as clubs. All day the fighting surged back and forth, with ground being taken, held for an hour, then lost in a counterattack, only to be retaken again. As evening fell, nothing significant had been gained by either side, and the forces retired to whatever makeshift lines they could form before darkness fell.

Grateful for the opportunity at last to get some rest, men from both sides of the bloody conflict soon found that even the darkness would not allow them to escape the suffering and misery that had marked the day's terrible events. A new enemy now unleashed its wrath upon the wounded and dying who lay in the tangles and wood-choked gullies of the confusing battlefield. This new enemy was—fire!

In the bitter fighting just before dark, the musket flashes had started a number of small fires that now erupted into a full-fledged forest fire. Caught in the path of the blaze were the dead and wounded of both armies who were strewn all through the woods. Soon the magnitude of the situation became fully known as men screamed in agonizing pain as the flames began to consume the wounded and dying. Piercing cries and pleas for death echoed through the darkness. The air began to fill with the smell of burning flesh. It was more than even these hardened veterans of either side could stand.

Sergeant William Neil of the 27th Virginia Regiment of the famed Stonewall Brigade went to his commander, Lieutenant Colonel Charles L. Hayes, and requested that the colonel attempt to arrange a truce so that both sides might join forces to remove the wounded from the path of the fire. The colonel agreed and told the sergeant to organize volunteers for the dangerous task while he made arrangements with Union forces holding the positions across from them.

Among the Virginia volunteers was a young Rebel soldier named Joshua Bates, the son of a Baptist minister who had disowned his only son for engaging in this awful war.

The truce arranged, Sergeant Neil and ten volunteers put their weapons aside and went to join a Union sergeant and ten of his unarmed men in a clearing between the lines. The two squads braved the heat and flames of the forest fire to bring out their wounded brothers-in-arms, without regard to the color of their uniforms.

The mission of mercy continued for over an hour, with the wounded hastily carried back to the clearing, where others tended them and moved them farther back behind the lines. But even with this effort, not all could be rescued. The screams of the less fortunate carried on the night air filled with smoke, heat, and the smell of burning flesh. Still the rescuers returned time after time in an effort to save as many as possible from such a terrible fate.

Weary from running back and forth and suffering from heat exhaustion, Private Bates and three others returned once more into the flames to retrieve a soldier screaming that his pants were on fire. Locating the man, Bates dropped to his knees and threw dirt onto the burning pants to put out the fire.

As the rescuers prepared to pick up the wounded man, they heard a cracking sound and saw a towering tree in all its fiery glory crash down between them and the only way out of the fire. The rescuers themselves were now surrounded by the roaring blaze that quickly began to close in on them. There were no avenues of escape, and any hope of rescue was impossible. One of the soldiers cried out, "My God! We're all going to die!"

Kneeling beside the soldier with the burnt pants legs, Private Bates encouraged those around him to do the same and join hands. When they did, he began to pray.

"Oh, Lord, our task this night has been a mighty one. We have risked all to save our fellow man. Would you now reward us for showing compassion by committing us to this fiery furnace? We beseech you, Almighty God ... come to our aid in this time of great need. In your name, we ask. Amen."

From their tightly-knit group within the surrounding flames, the four men saw a lone figure appear beyond the fire. It was a figure of unusual height, dressed not in a uniform but in what appeared to be a baggy sackcloth robe. The figure raised a hand and called to the men surrounded by the flames, "Come out, hurry! Come this way and bring your wounded brother."

Hesitant at first, the men looked at one another, then back to the figure who now seemed to move directly into the flames, yet was unharmed by the fire. Again the calm and gentle voice told them to follow him. Still uncertain, but having little to lose, the four men picked up the wounded soldier and began moving toward the figure in the fire. As they neared the flames the figure turned and walked away. As it did, a sudden wind swept over the men and the wall of flame seemed to split apart, leaving an opening of some twenty feet. Without delay, Bates and the others hurried through the exit. Within seconds they were free of the raging fire that immediately consumed the very area in which they had been kneeling only minutes before.

Scurrying clear of the heat and flames, the men placed the wounded man on the ground and looked around for the figure who had encouraged them to escape certain death, but there was no one there. They were the only ones in the immediate area. The mysterious figure had vanished.

In a letter to his parents following the Battle of the Wilderness, young Joshua Bates told of what had happened that night in the fiery woods, of how two armies at war had put aside their differences for a time to save not a Yankee or a Rebel, but their fellow man. Bates was convinced that his prayer for their rescue had been answered by the intervention of one of God's angels on that night.

Private Nathan Riddle, a member of the Union's 19th Massachusetts, was with Bates that night and likewise wrote of the experience to his parents in Boston. Although not a highly religious man, Riddle could not explain the events of that night, other than to suggest that there had to have been some type of divine intervention.

Joshua Bates survived the Civil War and returned home, where he became a Baptist minister and was often requested to relate his story of the miracle in the bloody Battle of the Wilderness. He passed away quietly in his sleep in December 1913, convinced that his life and those of the men with him that night had been spared by an angel of the Lord.

The Protector

A PERSON WOULD have a very difficult time convincing Susan Shiply of Charleston, South Carolina, that angels are not real.

On the night of October 15, 1993, the twenty-three-year-old corporate secretary had worked late completing an important draft of a presentation her company would be presenting to a client the following morning. It was well past nine in the evening when she finished and took the elevator to the first floor. Charles, the security guard, let her out the double-glass front doors and as always kept a watchful eye on her until she was safely in her car and driving away. Charles waved to her as she drove past, locked the doors again, and returned to his desk.

Susan smiled to herself as she exited the parking lot. Charles was in his late fifties. A kind-hearted, caring man that always had a smile and a kind word for everyone he met. He was particularly fond of Susan. She reminded him of his niece. It had taken Susan a year to finally convince the kindly man that he didn't have to walk her to her car every night. But the night Charles finally gave in to her request, he did so reluctantly and not before giving her a lecture of sorts. "Now, these are dangerous times, young lady," he had said, "and there are a lot of evil people roaming around out there in the dark. It makes me plenty nervous I'll tell you sure. Why, I pray for you to get home safe every time I see you leavin' after dark. Figure it can't hurt having a few angels travelin' along with you."

Susan Shiply came from a religious family and had attended church with her family faithfully every Sunday while living at home. But then came college and a career and somewhere along the way Susan had drifted away from going to church. There just never seemed to be enough time for it. She hadn't really thought much about that until Charles had mentioned praying and the angels. Seeing him wave as she left, she was reminded of her promise to herself to start attending church again, even if it were only once or twice a month—of course, she had been saying that for three months now, but there always seemed to be so many other things that needed to be done on her time off.

As she waited for a stop light to change, Susan suddenly remembered that she needed some things from the store. But she had used what money she had in her purse for lunch that day. Glancing across the street, Susan saw a drive-through bank. It had an automatic teller machine. "Perfect," she sighed. "Those are the greatest things to come along in years."

The light changed and Susan turned into the drive and pulled up to the automatic teller machine. She removed her bank card, rolled down her window, and leaned over to insert the card but dropped it. "Oh, great, Susan. What a klutz."

The card had hit the curb next to the machine and landed under her car. Pulling forward a few feet, she opened her car door and walked back to pick it up. Just as she was about to put the card in the machine she felt a presence behind her. When she turned around her heart nearly stopped. There, standing only a few feet away, were three rough-looking teenage boys. They wore shirts with the sleeves torn off at the shoulder, ragged jeans, and bandannas tied around their heads. The largest of the three had a cigarette hanging from the corner of his mouth and was grinning at her in a sadistic sort of way as he looked her up and down. "Yeah—you're lookin' fine, mama! Don't let us stop you, honey. Go on, put your cart in there and punch up that old code for us, okay? We could use a few bucks, too."

"Yeah, mama!" said another, "we get some bucks and we can really show you a good time tonight—all three of us!"

Fear gripped Susan's very soul at that moment. She knew what would happen, even if she did everything they asked. It was their eyes. These boys had more in mind than a simple robbery of a lone girl at a teller machine. "Oh, God, please . . ." she whimpered, struggling not to burst into tears.

"Yo," laughed one of the boys. "Hey man, she's calling on old man God himself. How 'bout that?"

"Okay with me," said the big one. "Long as the old boy's got his bank card with him, too."

They all laughed at the remark. That, and the thrill they were getting from watching Susan tremble. "Come on, mama! Get that number in there—you're makin' me hot shakin' that little bod of yours around like that." He took a step toward her and with a foul breath shouted, "Do it! Now, bitch!"

Shaking, Susan turned to the machine and inserted the card. Tears were streaming down her face as she tried to see the numbers. Suddenly, she saw Charles' face as clear as if he were standing right in front of her, and she heard his voice saying, "Do not fear—angels are with you."

The face and the words calmed her and she prayed, "Oh, Lord, I call upon you to grant me the protection of your angels in my time of need. I ask in thy namesake. Please help me."

"I don't hear no beepin', mama! You better get to punchin' those numbers," said the leader of the trio.

For a second, Susan's heart sank. She didn't know what she expected to come of the prayer, but whatever it was, it didn't happen. Resigned to her fate, Susan punched the first number. The lights around the bank and the teller machine blinked off and on for a second, then seemed to turn a light blue, casting an eerie glow over her car, the machine and the four people standing near it. Susan was terrified. She was afraid to turn around. She didn't know what was happening.

The brightness of the blue light suddenly intensified. There was a loud popping sound and everything went off. The light was gone. Everything had been pitched into darkness—everything that is, except Susan. A sudden calmness passed over her. The fear was gone and a voice told her to turn and face her enemies. When she did turn, she saw the faces of the three boys. They were masked in cowering fear. What did they see? Susan looked around, but saw no one, yet, the boys were backing away, as if some giant monster or nightmare were about to engulf them. Something told Susan to take a step toward them. As she did, the three boys screamed a blood curdling scream and took off running as fast and as far away as they could.

Once they were gone, the faint light that had surrounded Susan faded and the normal lights came back on. Running to her car, Susan quickly started the motor and drove straight home. Once inside the safety of her apartment. Susan fell to her knees at her bed and wept, thanking God for her deliverance from a fate worse than death and vowing to renew her bond with Him and His angels. To this day, Susan Shiply has not missed a single Sunday service at her church—and it is not likely she ever will.

Like the Lion and the Lamb

CHUCK FARINGTON HAD grown up living the life more than a few boys in America had dreamed about. He had grown up a cowboy in the badlands country of South Dakota. Born and raised on a ranch, he had grown up with horses, cattle, ropes, and real cowboys—not the Hollywood version, but the real McCoy.

Contrary to popular belief, the life of a cowboy was, and still is, a hard one. Up at the crack of dawn, taking care of the stock on the ranch first, then mounting up for a long day in the saddle, mending fences, chasing down strays, or rounding up a herd for branding. These are but a few of the countless things they have to attend to every minute of every day. For Chuck it was a way of life, and one that he wouldn't trade with anyone, anywhere.

Chuck's grandfather had built their ranch from scratch. He had started with a two-room sod home in the middle of the vast Dakota badlands during a time when names like Crazy Horse, Sitting Bull, and George Armstrong Custer were as common as Johnny Carson and Bill Clinton are to us today. Where that sod house had been built with such loving care, now stood a two-story, six-bedroom house. Ten rib-thin cows had been the start of what was now a thousand head of some of the finest cattle in the Dakotas. This was the legacy that had been left to forty-year-old Chuck Farington with the passing of his father and mother in a car accident in 1959.

One cool morning in April 1960, Chuck had breakfast with his foreman and crew. They discussed the work that had to be done, then went out to saddle up their horses. Ford and Chevy trucks made good television commercials and were a nice convenience to have, but were of little use in the high country of the Dakotas when it came to rounding up stock that had wandered up into the rocks and canyons.

Chuck and three of his hired hands would work the west sector while the foreman and the others searched out the east side of the canyons. By noon the sun was shining down warm and bright and it was turning out to be a pretty nice day all the way around. Setting his horse on a rise, Chuck looked out over the countryside and as he often did, thought of the first time his father had brought him up into the high country. They had set their horses in that very spot. He remembered his father's words that day. "Son, there are a lot of folks out there in the world that don't believe in God. Just once, I'd like to bring those folks up here and let them see all of this from this very spot. Anyone that could look out over all this and not believe in a greater power must not have any kind of life at all. This is God's country, boy—and don't you ever forget that. You ever want to talk to him—you must rise your head and look up. He'll be there. I guarantee it."

By late afternoon, Chuck and his boys had gathered up nearly a hundred head of cattle. Chuck told the others to drive them back down to the flatlands. He'd be along shortly. There was one other place he wanted to look. Watching the others make their way down the mountain, Chuck wheeled his horse and walked him toward a shallow gully lying just below a steep ridge. He was certain there were at least a couple of cattle down in that gully.

Chuck had just passed under the shadow of the ridge when his horse suddenly reared up and began to snort wildly. "Whoa, old girl! What is it?"

His question was answered within seconds as the low growling roar of a mountain lion echoed off the walls of the gully, frightening the horse even more. "Easy, girl! Easy!" shouted Chuck as he tried to pull his Winchester rifle from the saddle. But the horse wanted no part of it. This time it reared even higher and twisted at the same time, throwing Chuck from the saddle and down a slight incline. There was a sudden pain in his leg. Without looking, Chuck knew the leg was broken. His horse, free of its rider, raced back up the gully and over the hill, taking the Winchester with it.

Chuck was alone now—or was he? Where was the mountain lion? His eyes darted across the rocks and cliffs searching for the cause of his present predicament, but he could not see anything. "Probably looking right down my neck this very minute," said Chuck, struggling to ignore the pain in his leg. It would be getting dark soon and with the darkness would come the cold—the near freezing cold of an April night in the Dakota mountains. And Chuck was far from being dressed for that. His only hope was that his jughead of a horse would head straight for the ranch. When the crew saw the empty saddle they'd be out looking for him. But how long would that take?

As the minutes slipped into hours, Chuck's leg began to swell, but the pain had eased. As long as he didn't move he was all right. But the temperature was beginning to drop and Chuck was beginning to feel it. If they didn't find him before dark, they'd have to wait until morning to try again. The terrain was just too rugged, making it perilous for both horse and rider. Chuck wasn't sure he could survive the night in these mountains.

As the sun disappeared beyond the mountains, and darkness closed in around him, Chuck knew real fear for the first time. Remembering his father's words, he looked up into the broad sky that was quickly filling with stars and prayed.

"Well, God, here we are. Just you and me and some old mountain lion that would like to make me his supper, but I sure wouldn't care for that myself. I don't mean to impose on you, but if you could somehow spare a little time I sure could use some help here. I've always tried to be an honest man and made sure you were given your due for all this beauty you created around us, Lord. I sure would like to stay around and look at it a little longer. Your will be done, God. Amen."

As the hours passed the night got colder, and the pain in his broken leg became almost unbearable. Slowly Chuck felt himself slipping away into a whirlpool of darkness until finally he lost consciousness.

When Chuck came to, he was at the ranch in his own bed, with warm covers tucked in around him and his leg in a cast supported by a pole. His wife and foreman were sitting next to the bed and smiled a greeting as he tried to remember how he had got home. But he couldn't remember a thing. It was then that his foreman told him how they had come to find him.

The riderless horse had come into the ranch as Chuck knew it would. They had immediately begun a search for their boss but with all the cattle tracks it was hard to backtrack the horse. When it got dark, they reluctantly turned back. Trying to find him in the dark would have been both dangerous, and like trying to find a needle in a haystack.

Near midnight, Chuck's horse had begun to

race around the corral and kick wildly at the fence. When the crew went out to see what was wrong with the animal, they saw the horse jump the fence, race off toward the hills, then come back to the front of the bunkhouse and paw at the ground with its hooves. It did this several times before somebody finally realized that the horse was trying to get them to follow him.

Saddling their horses, the men followed the horse up into the mountains. As the foreman told the story, Chuck could only shake his head. His horse was a good one, but not really anything special. Chuck had not been able to teach it anything and even more surprising was the fact that the horse jumped the fence. The horse was not a jumper. "You trying to tell me that old jughead led you boys back to me?" asked Chuck.

"Well, not exactly, boss," said his foreman, scratching his head. "It got us in the general area all right, but that ain't how we found you."

Chuck pulled himself up in bed and stared at his foreman who had a strange look on his face. "Well, come on, Bob. Seems like you're going the long way around to cross a short fence. Just spit it out."

"Well sir, it was the strangest thing me and the boys ever saw. We come up around that ridge near the gully where we found you and it was so dark we wouldn't have seen you if we'd have rode right over you, but then—this old mountain lion just came walking out of the rocks and stared at us for a couple of minutes. Your horse went over toward him and the two of 'em just walked right down into that gully. When we followed 'em in we found the lion gone and your horse standing over you. Now, that's the honest-to-God truth, boss. All us boys saw it happen just like I said. How's a fellow explain somethin' like that?'' asked the foreman.

Chuck smiled and looking out his window at the mountains outlined against the night sky answered, ''He doesn't, Bob. He doesn't even try. He just says he's grateful and goes on as best he can, thanking the good Lord for each day he spends upon this earth.''

TENNESSEE

Flowers of Love Acknowledged

WHENEVER HAVEN CONNER of Chattanooga, Tennessee, sees a daisy she thinks of her close friend, Barbara. They were sorority sisters in college. After Barbara became engaged, she asked Haven to be her bridesmaid. Together they searched for a silverware pattern with daisies. At the wedding, Haven carried the yellow and white flowers up the aisle, and daisies adorned everything at the reception.

Even though she was now married, Barbara talked to Haven practically every day. Before long, Haven, too, was married, but that did nothing to separate these two friends. They still talked all the time and often went out together for dinner and a movie. Then one day a terrible thing happened. Haven allowed an argument between their husbands drive a wedge between them. They hardly ever talked, stopped celebrating their birthdays together and there were no more dinners out or Christmas cards exchanged. Suddenly they were no longer friends anymore. Haven knew in her heart she didn't want things this way, but kept putting off calling Barbara to make things right again. Then one day she learned that Barbara had died. She was totally shocked. Barbara was only thirty-eight years old.

Haven agonized over what had been left unsaid. One afternoon Haven slumped in a chair in her backyard, where she had hosted Barbara's wedding reception. "Oh God," she prayed, "I shall never forgive myself for not telling Barbara how sorry I am and how much I loved her."

Haven was stunned to hear a gentle voice from somewhere above her say, "Tell her now." Haven looked everywhere, but there was no one in sight. She was totally alone.

Haven broke down and began to pour out her heart, just as she and Barbara used to do in their college days. "You were the best friend I ever had," Haven said as she wept. "I'm so sorry." At that very moment, Haven had the strangest feeling that somehow Barbara had heard every word she had said. Regaining her composure, Haven went about her yard work, trimmed away some branches and mowed the lawn. That night she went to bed with a lighter heart. Her only regret—that she had not reached out to Barbara when she could have still responded.

The next morning, in a corner of the yard, sprouting up from the freshly mowed lawn Haven discovered an unexpected bouquet—a foot high clump of yellow and white daisies.

Pushing the Clouds Away

MARY CAROL NEWLAND is a paramedic. All her life all she had ever wanted to do was care for others. She felt that she had a God-given sixth sense for emergency situations. It was as if this was the work God himself wanted her to do. At one time Mary was employed by a firm called Aeromedics, Incorporated. One day they received a call from an insurance company in New York. One of their clients was vacationing in Acapulco, Mexico, and his eighteen-month-old son had been seriously injured. The child needed to be airlifted to a hospital in Houston as soon as possible. It could mean the difference between life and death. Mary assured the caller that she would have the child in Houston that night.

Aeromedics leased a ten-passenger, twin-engine King Air for the flight and would be flying out of the airport in Brownsville, Texas. Mary arrived at the airport with all the equipment she

needed to care for the boy on the flight. While
the equipment was loaded, Mary discussed the
flight with her pilot, Bob Sizemore. Bob said the
weather looked good all the way to Acapulco.
Accompanying them would be Ron Bonsall, Mary's flight coordinator, and Salvador Robles, her
aide and translator.

Bob had been right. The flight to Mexico was
picture perfect, but upon their arrival things began to go wrong as soon as they landed. There
was no ambulance waiting as she had requested.
They waited an hour, then decided to take a cab
to the hospital twenty miles away. Another problem arose when the customs agents refused to
allow the medical equipment to be removed
from the airport. They were suspicious and felt
that they were going to try and sell the expensive
equipment without paying the customs charges
that were required. Salvador argued on their behalf and after several heated arguments finally
persuaded the customs people to allow them to
leave with the much-needed equipment.

At the hospital they found the small boy in a
hospital bed, his head wrapped in bandages and
his parents very distraught. The boy's injury had
been a freak accident that had occurred at an ice
cream parlor. He had been struck in the head by
a ceiling fan when his father had hoisted him up
on his shoulders inside the store. Doctors had
performed surgery to determine the extent of the
boy's injuries and now infection had set in. The
boy was suffering seizures.

The boy was conscious and his mother explained that he was terrified. He refused to let the doctors or nurses touch him. But when he saw Mary, he struggled to sit up and opened his arms to her, wanting her to pick him up, as if he knew he would be safe with her.

Back at the airport, they lost another precious hour because the parents did not have their passports and papers in order. Again Salvador's services were needed to convince the officials that they were not kidnaping a Mexican baby. They finally agreed to allow the plane to leave with the baby, but the father would have to remain behind until their papers and passports were properly completed.

The flight landed back at Brownsville, Texas, at 9:00 P.M. Along the way, the baby had suffered a series of seizures and vomited several times. Sal left them at Brownsville and another pilot, Bob Stembock, came aboard. By FAA rules, Bob Sizemore had used his allotted twelve hours of flying time for the day.

Before they took off for the second leg of their trip, Bob Sizemore, who remained on the flight to serve as co-pilot, approached Mary. They now had another problem. "Mary, there are severe thunderstorms ahead and they've spotted tornadoes near Houston," said Bob. "We think we should wait until morning."

"No," said Mary, seeing the concerned look on the face of the baby's mother. "We've got to get this child to Houston."

"I don't think we should, Mary," said Sizemore. "We could run into a twister on the way."

"The weather is outside the parameters set by the FAA," said the new pilot, Bob Stembock.

Mary knew both men; they were veteran pilots. But now she was getting that feeling—that sixth sense. Mary seemed to know something they did not.

"Okay," she said. "So we run into bad weather . . . the Lord will get us through."

Both pilots looked uncomfortable with Mary's answer to the present problem.

"I know it sounds crazy," said Mary, "but trust me. We've got an injured child here, and God's not going to let anything else happen to him. He will protect us, I promise you!"

Even as she spoke, Mary's sixth sense seemed to grow stronger. The pilots looked as if they wanted to believe her, but they were still skeptical.

Mary's patience was growing thin and time was vital. "Look," she said abruptly, "if you guys won't fly, then I'll find another pilot who will."

Bob Stembock spoke with an uneasy laugh, "Hey, I wouldn't go out in a snowstorm for milk, but if it's a matter of getting someone to a hospital, well . . ."

"We just wanted you to know the weather situation," added Bob Sizemore. "If you're ready, we'll go."

They departed Brownsville at 9:30, under a full moon in a deceptively clear sky. Twenty minutes later, they found themselves in the middle of a storm. The plane veered and yawed like a leaf in the wind. Lightning leaped across the clouds a mere thirty feet from the plane. The two pilots looked tense. Sizemore pored over charts and talked with Houston control while Stembock fought to keep the plane on course.

"I'll tell you, Mary Carol," said Sizemore, looking back over his shoulder, "I've been in some pretty rough weather before, but this one beats everything."

As if on cue, the plane was suddenly caught in a heartstopping downdraft. The baby's mother was praying, and Ron Bonsall, sitting across from Mary, seemed a little pale. Again the plane dropped suddenly and lurched violently to the right. Mary was quickly losing her own courage. She began to wonder if she had acted rashly. What if she had misjudged God's will and her sixth sense? She could be responsible for the death of six people. She clutched the baby close to her and prayed.

"Dear Lord, protect us. Send your angels to keep this plane in the air."

The plane continued to pitch and buck, but at least now, Mary felt calmer. She knew that God was in control. The flight from Brownsville to Houston usually takes one hour and forty-five minutes, but this night it took two and a half hours.

It was near midnight when Bob brought the plane down at the Houston airport. An ambulance was waiting and they quickly loaded the baby and his mother inside and took off for the hospital where doctors were waiting to receive them.

As Mary stood watching the ambulance drive away with its siren blaring and its lights flashing, she knew she was where God wanted her to be—and that He had been faithful in guiding them through the storm.

Afterwards, Bob Sizemore came up to her. "Mary, I've been a pilot for over forty years, but I've never seen anything like that!"

"It was pretty rough," said Mary.

"No, no!" he protested. "It sounds a little crazy, I know, but with all hell breaking loose all around us up there, suddenly a kind of chasm—a canyon—opened up in the clouds in front of us. The clouds stood off on either side of us, and this canyon just kept opening up, opening up, all the way from south of Corpus Christi to Galveston."

Mary could feel the skin prickling on the back of her neck and arms. That sixth sense . . .

"I told you God would get us through," she said with a smile.

The baby boy fully recovered from his injury and today is doing fine.

UTAH

The Unseen Protector

CAROL CONNERS OF Provo, Utah, is a firm believer in guardian angels and has good reason to feel that way.

On a warm summer day in 1992, she was shopping with a girlfriend. They were searching for the perfect wedding gift for Carol's sister who was getting married that weekend. Stopping for lunch at a small restaurant off Main Street, the two girls were discussing the wedding and the conversation eventually came around to religion. Carol's friend, Clair, was not the most religious person Carol knew. As a matter of fact, Clair was more of a borderline agnostic—a person who does not totally deny the existence of God, but believes it is impossible for anyone to prove that He does exist.

Carol on the other hand had been raised by parents who were highly involved in their church's activities and saw to it that their children were as well. One of the first things Carol had done when arriving at her new job in the city of Provo was to find a church she could join and attend regularly.

Carol could see that the conversation was beginning to make Clair feel a little uncomfortable and changed the subject. But made a mental note to one day discuss, in earnest, Clair's feelings and doubts about God.

The two friends had just finished their meal and were relaxing with a cup of coffee when suddenly, Carol felt a slight breeze brush across the back of her neck and a voice whispered an urgent warning to her. "Carol, move away from the window—do it now!"

Instinctively, she turned to see who was standing behind her, but there was no one there. Clair stared at her friend for a second then asked, "What's wrong, Carol?"

Carol realized that Clair had not heard the voice, which again issued its warning, this time in a more forceful tone. "Carol! Take your friend and move away quickly—do it now!"

Carol suddenly pushed her chair back and reaching across the table, grabbed Clair's arm and began pulling her away from the window and back toward the main dining area. Clair, shocked at the sudden move, looked at her friend as if the woman was crazy. Others in the restaurant stared at the couple as Clair shouted, "My God, Carol—what's wrong with you!"

Seconds later a car came crashing through the plate glass window and halfway into the restaurant. Beneath the front bumper of the car lay the shattered remains of a table and chairs—the very same table that Clair and Carol had been sitting at only moments before.

Clair stood with her mouth open and in total shock. "My God, Carol—how did you know?"

She squeezed her friend's hand and with a smile answered, "My guardian angel warned me."

Clair looked at her a moment then back to the crumpled table and chairs. "Carol, would you mind if I went to church with you this weekend?" she asked.

VIRGINIA

An Angel's Drift

CHARLES LEGGETT WAS a junior at Virginia Military Institute, a small college located in the beautiful Shenandoah Valley. It was September and the weather was remarkably comfortable for that late in the year.

One Sunday afternoon, Charles and a small group from his dorm decided it would be a perfect day to go rappelling. There were some great cliffs for the sport not far from the campus.

The young men arrived at the site shortly after lunch and rigged their equipment. The cliffs stood around one hundred and twenty feet high and overlooked the Maury River. They selected a landing area about a hundred feet below the top of the cliffs and rigged a safety line that led back to the top on one side. Once everything was ready, Charles, standing at the bottom of the landing area, stared up at the top of the cliffs and was overcome with a sudden desire to show-off a little bit for his dorm brothers. Leaving the safety line, Charles crossed the landing area and began climbing the cliffs on his own. Like most college students his age, he hadn't given much thought to his own mortality, therefore, he thought nothing of climbing without a safety line or a helmet. Having been rappelling a number of times, Charles should have known better, but the idea of falling never entered his mind.

Soon, moving slowly upward and finding foot- and handholds along the way, he was within five feet of the top. Feeling confident and somewhat cocky at his success, Charles shifted his weight and was reaching for a final handhold when he felt the small ledge he was standing on crumble and fall away, leaving him hanging by one hand on a small outcrop of rock. Desperately he tried to find something to grab onto, but his last handhold was lost as the outcrop of rock also broke away and he began to fall. Moments before he blacked out, Charles felt a hand grab his arm. Then everything went blank.

Charles estimates that he lost consciousness for five to ten minutes. When he slowly began coming around he found that he was sitting on a ledge with his back to the cliff, less than twenty feet above the river. His left leg was twisted painfully underneath him. He was scratched up some, but otherwise he was okay.

Charles looked up the face of the cliff and found the spot from where he had fallen—it was ninety feet above him. His body was now turned, so that he no longer faced the cliff, and he had also fallen fifteen feet diagonally—and landed in a seated position!

Slowly and carefully, Charles made his way down from the ledge, across the landing area, then up the safety line to the top. His friends were shocked to see that he had suffered only minor scratches from his ordeal. They had already sent someone back to the school for medical help. None of them could arrive at a logical explanation for his miraculous lack of serious injury or his safe landing on the ledge ninety feet below.

Charles never thought twice about the answer. Raised in a solid Christian home, Charles had always been a believer in guardian angels. That Sunday afternoon, in his junior year at VMI, Charles had an opportunity to experience the presence of his guardian angel.

WASHINGTON

The Slide for Life

IN THE SUMMER of 1989, Roger Harris and Tom Craig, students at the University of Washington, were spending their summer break working for the Washington State Park Service. The area they were working was around Mount Olympus in Olympic National Park. It was rugged country, but exactly what the two boys had wanted. Both athletes, they figured this would be the perfect job and the perfect place to keep them in shape during the summer.

One morning they were working replacing timbers along one of the hiking trails when they heard a woman's scream for help. The cry was coming from somewhere farther up the trail. Dropping their equipment, the two boys raced up the twisting trail toward the cries for help. Rounding a curve they found a middle aged woman on her knees, her face in her hands, crying.

Tom knelt down next to her and asked, "What's wrong? What's happened?"

The woman looked up at them and a sign of hope leapt into her eyes as she pointed across the trail and said, "My son! It's my son—he fell over the edge of a cliff—he's gone! I know he's gone."

While Tom cared for the woman, Roger rushed to where she had been pointing. The brush along this point of the trail was deceptive. It hid the sudden drop-off that lay only a few feet through the brush. Kneeling carefully, Roger leaned out over the ledge and looked down, expecting to see the body of the woman's son smashed upon the rocks below. But there was nothing there. Roger was about to go back to the trail when he heard a soft whimper coming up from the rocks. Leaning back over the ledge a second time, he yelled, "Is there anyone down there?"

"Yes! Help me. I can't hold on much longer. Help me."

Tom was now at Roger's side and asked what was going on. Roger told him he could hear the boy, but couldn't see him. From what the voice had said he was barely holding on. He needed help fast. Tom told Roger that the boy was only ten years old. Neither of the boys had any equipment with them and it would take too long to go back to their truck and call for help. Roger looked over the ledge again. It was a straight drop-off for about thirty feet, with a tree-covered slope jutting out just below that for another forty feet or so, then another drop-off. Searching the

area, Roger saw a dead tree lying near the cliff.
The two boys pulled it over to the spot and began easing it over the edge. They had to be careful because they weren't sure where the boy
was—if the log slipped away from them it could
hit the boy and send him down the slope and
over the final drop-off.

Roger, the more experienced climber of the
two, went over the ledge and began working his
way down the dead tree. Suddenly, one of the
limbs gave way and Roger went sliding haphaz-
ardly down the tree, landing hard on the slope,
and then tumbling end over end toward the major drop-off. Above, Tom watched in horror as
his friend rolled toward certain death and there
was nothing he could do to help. "Oh, God!" he
cried out, "please help him!"

Roger clawed and grabbed for anything to
stop his momentum but his weight worked
against him and he continued his slide toward
the edge and a three hundred foot drop-off. Suddenly, just as he saw his legs extend out into
open space, Roger felt something, or someone,
grab hold of his shirt and he came to a dead stop
in the dirt. His feet and legs were extending out
over the ledge—another four feet and he would
have went hurtling into space. Carefully, Roger
eased himself back away from the edge of the
dropoff. His hands were shaking and sweat
poured from his face. He had never known fear
like this. Looking around, he tried to figure out
what had stopped him from going over the edge.
There were no trees or rocks along the route of

his slide, yet he had stopped just short of falling to his death—or rather been stopped—by a sudden jerk on his shirt—but by whom? And from where?

From above, Tom yelled down to him that two other rangers had arrived and that they had a rope with them. Where was the boy? Roger looked back up the slope and saw the frightened little boy clinging to a tree stump underneath the overhang of the top ledge. Climbing back up the slope, he managed to persuade the child that he could let go of the stump. Tom tossed the rope down and Roger swiftly fashioned a sling and placed it around the boy. Once he was on top, the rangers tossed the rope down and Roger climbed up, more than happy to be away from the three hundred foot drop-off that had nearly claimed his life.

After the woman hugged her son and kissed Roger on the cheek about a hundred times, the other two rangers took the woman and her son back down the trail. Roger stood looking out over the slope. He could clearly see the slide marks in the dirt where less than twenty minutes ago his body had been sliding into eternity. Without looking at his friend, he asked, "Tom, did you see what stopped me from going over the edge down there?"

"Why, no, Roger. Matter of fact, I thought you were gone for sure. Then, you just seemed to stop dead in the dirt right there near the edge. Man, you're either the luckiest guy in the world or the angels love a hero. I don't know which."

Roger wasn't sure either, but as he walked away from that site he had a feeling that the score was now, for today anyway: angels—one, the Grim Reaper—zero.

WEST VIRGINIA

Making Change

FROM DENISE WATERS comes an interesting story to which I can relate, as I am sure many of us can. It is a short story, but one that shows how God's messengers work his will, answer many of our questions, and, if not immediately, eventually surprise us in a way that allows us to know that we are heard.

Denise is a seventeen-year-old church member, who held a part-time job and attended services faithfully. One Sunday the young lady arrived at church and while waiting for services to begin she figured the amount of her tithe that was due for that day. According to her figures she was obliged to donate a total of seventeen dollars as her offering. Opening her purse she realized that all she had was a twenty dollar bill. As the offering plate was passed along the aisle Denise hesitated for a moment, then dropped the twenty into the plate and said silently, whimsically, "Well, Lord, I'm really only supposed to offer seventeen. But you can keep the change. After all, I guess you can't make change for a twenty."

Then, surprisingly, Denise heard a still voice say, "Your Lord can do anything. All you have to do is ask."

She had whispered the remark so quietly that no one could have possibly heard her. Denise glanced around to see who had spoken, but all she saw were other members sitting quietly, silently praying. Looking to the front she whispered, "No, Lord, it's Yours. Put it to good use."

Again the voice spoke, "He can do anything."

Finally, Denise whispered, "Okay, Lord, I have to admit my finances are awfully tight right now. I need every penny for my college savings account. If You could return my three dollars change, that would be great."

As she left the church, Denise couldn't help but laugh to herself. How would God ever fulfill this request?

Sunday passed, as did Monday and Tuesday. Denise was ready to forget her three dollar church-pew dialogue. But then on Wednesday the manager of the restaurant where she worked came over to her and said, "Here's a little bonus. Last month's sales exceeded our projections."

He reached over and placed an envelope in her hand. When Denise opened it, she found six crisp, new, one dollar bills. She had cast her three dollars upon the waters and they had returned double. Smiling, she thought, If the Lord can make change for a twenty, He can certainly change my life.

And He had—all for the better.

WISCONSIN

A Four-Word Phrase

IN 1985 DEBORAH ROSE, of Jefferson, Wisconsin, was working as a waitress at a local restaurant. Tuesday nights their special was fried chicken. This particular night few customers had ordered the special and there was quite a bit of chicken left over. "Deb, take some of that chicken home if you want," said the manager. What the heck, she thought. It would make a great late night snack if she got hungry. The chicken was greasy, so Deborah wrapped it in plastic, placed it in a small box, and put it in her purse.

The last few customers lingered longer than usual and by the time they closed, Deborah was late getting to her bus stop and missed the last bus going in her direction. It was late, and she didn't exactly look forward to walking home through deserted Milwaukee streets, but she had little choice. She didn't make much at her job and could ill afford the price of a cab. As she began

her long walk, Deborah said a silent prayer and
began to sing a hymn. God would see her home
safely.

But He didn't. A man with a knife leaped out
of the shadows, pushed her down a dark side
street, and spoke in foul-mouthed terms of what
he planned to do to her once they reached his
place on Brady Street. Why had God forsaken
her?

Despite her anger, she kept praying. And then,
from out of nowhere, and in a voice that only
she heard, came four words. They were very
clear, very firm. "Debbie, eat your chicken."

What! thought Debbie. Am I losing my mind?

Again the strange voice said, "Debbie, eat your
chicken!"

As she was bring dragged along, she pulled
out a chicken breast, and began struggling with
all the wrappings. Crying too hard to get it un-
wrapped, she carried it in her hand. Soon, they
reached Brady Street.

In an alley across the street, two large dogs
were rummaging about in a pile of spilled trash
cans. Suddenly the dogs perked up their heads,
sniffed the air. Growling, baring their teeth, they
charged at the man and Debbie. Her attacker
quickly released her and fled.

The dogs did not lunge at her. They stood silently staring at the food in her hand. Debbie
wiped the tears from her eyes then quickly un-
wrapped the chicken. She tore off the meat and
threw it down. The dogs fought hungrily for it.

Dropping pieces every few yards, Debbie got

the stray dogs to follow her home. By the time she was safely inside, she had begun to understand. "Debbie, eat your chicken"—the chicken that had been wrapped too well to be smelled by even a dog. Yet, in her hand, it had worked a miracle.

WYOMING

The Heavenly Rider

JAKE FARNSWORTH IS a seventy-five-year-old man who has spent his life working cattle ranches from the Dakotas to Montana and Nebraska to Wyoming. He is one of the few real cowboys left that experienced the early hardships of the vast, rugged country of a young state called Wyoming. He remembers the harsh, bitter winters that killed cattle and men alike in those early days—and still does on occasion. Although not much of a church-going man, Jake was a firm believer in God and his power. There was one incident in particular that occurred in 1938 that reaffirmed the cowboy's faith and instilled it in him forever.

It was a young nineteen-year-old Jake Farnsworth who rode the range at that time. Young though he may have been, he was a hard worker and a natural horseman who seemed to be born to the cowboy way of life. Highly respected by fellow cowboys twice his age for his determination and stick-to-it attitude, he was well liked by everyone in the outfit.

One morning, he and a cowboy named Slim "Highpockets" Weaver, so named because of his six-foot-six height, were rounding up some cattle along the south sector of a seven-thousand acre spread when Slim's horse reared up suddenly, tossing Slim into some rocks. Jake pulled a pistol and shot a snake which had been the cause of the accident. Between the snake and the gunshot, Slim's horse had had enough and took off for parts unknown.

A quick check of Slim showed that he had a broken leg, a broken arm, and possibly a broken back. Jake did what he could to make his partner comfortable and tried to figure out what to do. They were a long way from the ranch and not knowing if Slim's back was broken, Jake was afraid to lift him to put him aboard his horse. The only answer was to run for help, but that meant leaving Slim alone with two broken limbs and unable to move. It was pretty rough country. What if Jake couldn't find his way back to this spot? What if it got dark before help could head back? There were more than a few critters that roamed the range after dark. A helpless man would seem like a pretty easy meal for some of them. Jake pondered the matter for awhile then decided he had no choice. He would have to go for help.

Pulling his rifle from his saddle, Jake placed it beside Slim along with a box of ammunition. He told Slim to wait for an hour, then start firing off one round every half hour. That way they could locate him if it got dark before they came for him. Slim agreed, but it was clear to Jake that the man was in a lot of pain. He wasn't sure the cowboy could stay conscious that long. As Jake started to leave, Slim asked if he was going to die. Jake knelt down beside him and said, "Heck, Slim, God ain't about to let you die. He needs every cowboy he can get out here to take care of the place for him. Now don't you worry none. He'll be with you. You won't be alone, Slim."

Bidding his friend so-long and swearing that he'd be back, Jake mounted up and rode at breakneck speed for the ranch and help. Along the way, Jake found himself praying as the wind blew in his face. "Lord, he's a God fearin' man and a darn good one at that. Watch over him while I'm gone and don't let him feel that he's all alone. I'd appreciate it. Thank ya."

It took Jake just over an hour to reach the ranch. A crew and a wagon were ready in ten minutes and they were on their way back. That was good time, but one would not have thought so listening to Jake shouting and screaming at everyone to quit dragging their feet and get a move on.

Jake was confident that he could find the spot where Slim was, but what he hadn't counted on was the thunderstorm that suddenly blew up out of nowhere. The sky went dark. Thunder and lightning began to flash and boom and the rain came down in buckets, slowing their progress. It was getting pretty bad when the foreman rode up to Jake and said, "Jake, you can't find nobody in this storm. We'll have to hole up and wait it out."

Jake didn't want to hear that. "No! We can't do that, boss. Slim's hurt too bad. Every minute we wait is a minute he don't have. We got to keep goin'."

The foreman pointed out in front of him, into the curtain of driving rain. "You tellin' me you can see where we're goin' through that? Jesus, Jake, there ain't no way we can find him in this mess."

Jake leaned forward in his saddle and strained his eyes. The boss was right of course. He couldn't see thirty yards in front of him, let alone find a ridge along the south sector. They'd be lucky to stumble onto the south sector in this storm.

Jake's heart dropped. Somewhere out there in this downpour was his friend and he had promised he'd be back for him. Now, they could only wait and hope the storm stopped soon. "Lord," said Jake, "This'll be twice I talked to You in one day. You and me know that's a record. But, Slim's my friend and You just got to help us find him. I'm askin' You to give us a hand—and I'm askin' You with a please at the end. Amen."

The foreman was about to end the search when a bolt of lightning lit up the sky and through the rain Jake saw what he thought was a rider. He was on a white horse and seemed to be beckoning for Jake to follow him.

Jake shook his head and wiped at his eyes, then looked again. The horse and rider were still there and the man was still waving them forward. The foreman was sitting right next to Jake and looking in the same direction, but he did not seem to see the horse or the rider beckoning Jake on. At that moment, Jake Farnsworth felt his horse take off on its own and knew in his heart that there was an unseen power at work.

"Come on, boys!" he yelled as loud as thunder. "Follow me! I know where Slim is and it's not far."

The foreman grumbled, but picked up the yell for everyone to ride. And it was not a long ride. Fifteen minutes later they found Slim among the rocks. Judging from the empty shell casings around him, he had been firing the rifle, but the thunder and lightning had made the attempt a useless effort.

Jake left his horse in the rain, looking for any sign of the white horse and the rider who he had followed to the exact spot where they found Slim, but both horse and rider were gone. Some of the outfit joked with Jake as they loaded Slim in the wagon. They'd have to start calling him Buffalo Bill, or better yet Kit Carson, after the way he had led them through a driving storm to a spot no bigger than an outhouse.

Stepping up to the wagon, Jake said, "Told you I'd be back, didn't I, partner."

Slim managed a smile through his pain and replied, "Yeah, you did, Jake—an' you told me I wouldn't be out here alone neither—an' you was right about that, too. 'Bout the time I was ready to give up on everything, I saw a man on a white horse sittin' off on the ridge watching me. Took my mind off my pain for quite a spell, too. Couple times I passed out—I could have swore he rode right up to me to make sure I was all right. Then the rain started and you all showed up. Darndest thing. Don't you think, Jake. You think I was just goin' loco?"

Jake shook his head, "No, partner. I saw him, too."

"Where'd he go, Jake?"

"I don't rightly know, Slim—but I think we'll be seein' him again someday. Till then, he's welcome on this range anytime."

Bibliography and Resources

Adler, Mortimer J. *The Angels and Us*, Macmillan: New York, 1982.

Anderson, Joan Webster. *Where Angels Walk*, Barton & Brett: Sea Cliff, New York, 1992.

Brewer, Reverend Cobham. *A Dictionary of Miracles*, Gale Research Company: Detroit, 1966.

Brittleston, Adam. *Our Spiritual Companions: From Angels and Archangels to Cherubim and Seraphim*, Floris Books: Edinburgh, Scotland, 1980.

Burnham, Sophy. *A Book of Angels*, Ballantine Books: New York, 1990.

————. *Angels Letters*, Ballantine Books: New York, 1991.

Davidson, Gustav. *A Dictionary of Angels*, Free Press: New York, 1980.

Graham, Billy. *Angels: God's Secret Agents*, Pocket Books: New York, 1975.

Hodson, Geoffrey. *The Brotherhood of Angels and Men*, Quest Books: Wheaton, Illinois, 1927.

MacGregor, Geddes. *Angels: Ministers of Grace*, Paragon House: New York, 1988.

Moolenburg, Hans C. *A Handbook of Angels*,

C. W. Daniel Company: Safron Walden, England, 1984.

Parisen, Maria. *Angels and Mortals*, Theosophical Publishing House: Wheaton, Illinois, 1990.

Ronner, John. *Do You Have a Guardian Angel?*, Mamre Press: Murfreesboro, Tennessee, 1985.

————. *Know Your Angels*, Mamre Press: Murfreesboro, Tennessee, 1993.

Wilson, Peter. *Angels*, Pantheon Books: New York, 1980.

ANGEL RESOURCES

Angel Collectors Club of America
16342 West 54th Avenue
Golden, Colorado 80403

Angel Watch Newsletter
P.O. Box 1362
Mountainside, New Jersey 07092
(Fee for annual subscription)

Marilynn's Angels
275 Celeste
Riverside, California 92507
(Sales, Angel Merchandise)

Mamre Press
107 Second Avenue
Murfreesboro, Tennessee 37130
(Has catalog with wide variety)

I AM ALWAYS interested in hearing from those who believe they have had an angelic experience, especially fellow military veterans who may wish to relate a happening or incident that occurred to them or a friend during wartime. If you would care to share those or any other stories with me, please feel free to write to me at P.O. Box 417, Ada, Oklahoma 74820.

Amazing and Inspiring True Stories of Divine Intervention

They are with us always...

ANGELS   72331-X/$4.99 US
  by Hope Price

ANGELS AMONG US   77377-5/$4.99 US/$5.99 Can
  by Don Fearheiley

They happen when you least expect them and need them most...

MIRACLES   77652-9/$4.99 US/$5.99 Can
  by Don Fearheiley

AMERICA'S MOST INSPIRATIONAL AUTHOR

BEYOND OUR SELVES
72202-X / $8.00 US/ $10.00 Can

TO LIVE AGAIN
72236-4/ $8.00 US/ $10.00 Can

A MAN CALLED PETER
72204-6/ $8.00 US/ $10.00 Can

SOMETHING MORE
72203-8/ $8.00 US/ $10.00 Can

THE HELPER
72282-8/ $8.00 US/ $10.00 Can

CATHERINE MARSHALL'S STORY BIBLE
69961-3/ $10.95 US/ $13.95 Can